Praise for Anxious with Jesus

"What Tiffany has done with this book is something of a marvel. Rather than being 40,000 feet above the topic and therefore inaccessible, or conversely, being so granular in her story that she excludes her readers, she writes her way to a middle space and invites us into the tension that actually marks the relationship between faith and mental health."

JUSTIN MCROBERTS Author of *Sacred Strides* and *It Is What You Make of It*. Host of the *@Sea Podcast*. Songwriter, Coach, Speaker, Everythinger

"Anxious with Jesus is a book today's Church desperately needs; a complex, nuanced exploration of how faith and mental illness intertwine. Through humour, personal anecdotes and spiritual insights, Tiffany shares a strikingly honest story of how her own anxiety shaped her life—and her faith. She peels back the curtain on what happens inside doctor's offices and therapy rooms, allowing readers a frank look at the reality of believers living with anxiety disorders, as well as their treatment within the Church. Uniquely positioned to share on this topic, Tiffany strikes the balance between grace and gentle challenge, offering opportunities for reflection and learning about how we all—as the broader Church—can better love and understand those struggling in our midst. This book should be at the top of your reading list. It's for anyone who has wondered 'What's wrong with me?' or 'Why hasn't God healed me?' as well as those who love them, and anyone in the Church who wants to understand. You won't be able to put it down."

MADELEINE SCHOLFIELD, Managing Editor and Podcast Co-host at Anxious Faith, a branch of Our Daily Bread Ministries

"By vulnerably sharing her own experience with Generalized Anxiety Disorder, Tiffany expresses a profound truth needed for the modern church: Intense mental health struggle and strong faith can coexist. This book is an "I see you" for those suffering with clinical anxiety as well as a guide for supportive people trying to help them."

CARRIE BOCK, LPC-MHSP, Host of *Christian Faith and OCD* Podcast

"Reading felt like an inspiring conversation with a close friend. Tiffany has provided an engaging memoir with the incisive punch of cultural commentary: Despite what culture or even some in church might say, you're not crazy nor do you necessarily lack faith if you're a Christian who struggles with your anxiety and mental health. Tiffany shares example after example where I continually found myself exclaiming, "No way, me too!" From her bodily symptoms of muscle tension to her obsessions over having enough faith, her discoveries are practical for countless others who find themselves navigating problems that are now well known—but often misunderstood. Her story is relatable for Christians, those with anxiety disorders, and anyone considering topics of mental health and the church. This book promises what is needed most in our current landscape: raw, truthful stories of suffering and overcoming that highlight hope in Jesus despite uncertainty. It shines light on systems of thought that are broken. It calls for what we need: truth and love, faith with works, and real care for the mind, body, and spirit. As Tiffany states, 'Jesus showed up to my therapy sessions and brought some special mud with him.' Jesus continues to open eyes spiritually, mentally, and emotionally for those who want to see."

JUSTIN HUGHES, MA, LPC Therapist, Writer, Anxiety and OCD Specialist, Faith & OCD Action Council

"As a follower of Jesus for the last 30 years, and a mental health professional for 15 of those, I have spent a lot of my life navigating the intersection of faith and mental illness. Tiffany's book is an inspired melding of the author's personal experiences with anxiety coupled with clinical best practices she has learned along the way. These experiences are thoughtfully infused with a lot of Jesus, humor, and vulnerability; creating a unique read that shines a light into the darkness and isolation mental illness often creates. Beyond just an interesting read, her book equips readers with actionable strategies to navigate their own anxiety or walk alongside others with greater compassion and understanding."

RAEELLEN KEENEY, Licensed Clinical Social Worker

"In Anxious with Jesus, Tiffany Ciccone invites us into a journey that is both deeply personal and profoundly needed in the church today. With honesty, wisdom, and faith, Tiffany weaves together her experience with Generalized Anxiety Disorder and her unwavering love for Jesus, offering a voice of solidarity to those who have felt alone in their struggles. This book does not offer quick fixes or easy platitudes—instead, it extends grace, reminding us that anxiety is not a failure of faith but a reality many faithful believers face. As a pastor, I am grateful for her courage in writing what the church desperately needs to hear. And as her friend, I am inspired and moved by her vulnerability. If you've ever wrestled with fear, doubt, or the tension between faith and mental health, this book and its author will be worthy companions for your journey towards healing."

DANNY QUIMLAT, MA Theological Studies, Lead Pastor at Restored Church South Bay

This book is so engaging—simultaneously informative and animated with personal stories—that I finished it in one sitting. I have an understanding and empathy that I didn't have before, and I'm thankful that this book will help churches, small groups, and followers of Jesus understand and love all those around them who are living with thorns like Tiffany's.

LUMA HADDAD, Associate Regional Director of San Diego Metro Young Life

Copyright ©2025 Things and Stuff by Tiffany Ciccone.

Cover and interior design by Anna Campbell.

Mere Christianity by C.S. Lewis copyright © 1942, 1943, 1944, 1952 C.S. Lewis Pte. Ltd.

Present Concerns by C.S. Lewis copyright © 1986 C.S. Lewis Pte. Ltd.

Extracts reprinted by permission.

All Scripture quotations, unless otherwise indicated, are taken from the Holy Bible, New International Reader's Version®, NIrV® Copyright © 1995, 1996, 1998, 2014 by Biblica, Inc.™ Used by permission of Zondervan. All rights reserved worldwide. www.zondervan.comThe "NIrV" and "New International Reader's Version" are trademarks registered in the United States Patent and Trademark Office by Biblica, Inc.™

Some personal names and identifying details have been changed to protect the privacy of the individuals involved.

IBSN 979-8-9927607-0-5 (paperback)

IBSN 979-8-9927607-1-2 (Ebook)

Library of Congress Control Number: 2025908754

ANXIOUS WITH JESUS

anxious
WITH JESUS

*a memoir from the messy intersection
of faith and mental illness*

TIFFANY CICCONE

*This book is dedicated to everyone who
has ever felt anxious and alone.*

TABLE OF CONTENTS

INTRODUCTION
Diagnosis: Alone ... 5

PART I: BEGINNINGS
1. Early Years ... 13
2. Onset ... 29
3. On Sinking and Saving ... 41

PART II: HELP
4. Diagnosis ... 57
5. What I Learned in Therapy ... 67
6. Verse ... 81
7. Medication ... 87
8. Version 2.0 ... 101

PART III: PRESSING ON
9. Over Overcoming ... 119
10. Redemption: The Power of Weakness ... 131
11. Speaking of Stigma ... 141
12. Sunday Mornings ... 157
13. Serving ... 167
14. Belonging and the Body ... 175

APPENDIX
Acknowledgments ... 189
Discussion Questions ... 191
Cognitive Journal Template ... 205
Endnotes ... 213
About the Author ... 223

intro

"If you cannot find the book you want to read, then you must write it."

TONI MORRISON

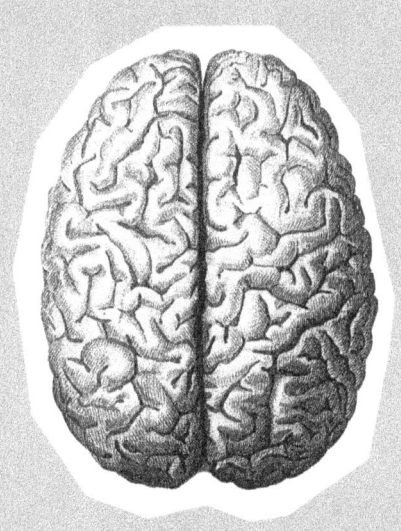

Diagnosis: Alone

INTRODUCTION: Diagnosis: Alone

The day I was diagnosed with Generalized Anxiety Disorder (GAD), I did what anyone would do—I Googled the crap out of it. At 24 years old, I sat on my bed, crouched over my laptop, and clicked around for articles and essays and blogs that might look me in my tired soul and say, "Hey, I get it. Me too. This *is* a thing. You're *not* alone."

It was 2007, and at first, I found more resources than I could scroll and click and read through. It was a great relief to learn that my malady had a name with bulleted symptoms that captured the thick, muddled chaos that had been hijacking my mind and body for the past year. WebMD assured me that it's normal for people with GAD to suffer "irrational, uncontrollable, spiraling thoughts of worry related to career, health, relationships, finance, and the future." It described the random physical sensations that came with—and at other times, without—thoughts of worry or fear. It was refreshing to hear other people describe my shallow breathing and tight chest, the swollen lump in my throat, and my sudden inability to think deeply. My diagnosis understood me, and it could help me be understood once again, both by myself and by others.

In that regard, I was no longer alone, but in another I felt more alone than ever. There was a part of me about which the internet was silent. It is the part, actually, that holds my entire self together. You see, Jesus was deep in my soul long before Generalized Anxiety Disorder came along and, in the words of my doctor, "broke my brain." With Jesus at the core of my beliefs and values, most of my anxious thoughts had "CHRISTIANITY" and "THEOLOGY" tattooed on their foreheads. They were massively entangled with my deep-seated relationship with Jesus.

I'd been attending church since forever, and while I'd heard plenty of sermons about anxiety, worry, and fear, I'd never heard anyone talk about anxiety like *mine*. And back in 2007, I had never heard of—let alone *met*—a Christian who admitted to having an anxiety disorder.

I knew, however, that I couldn't be the only believer with my struggle. Corinthians 10:13 assured me, "the temptations in your life are no different from what others experience." And as a lover of literature, I knew that nobody is all alone. Underneath it all, we are all far more similar than we realize.

And so as the sun sank lower, and my bedroom grew darker, I dug deeper into the interwebs to find my sisters and brothers who shared my burden. I needed to absorb what they had learned: I needed their wisdom and guidance and fellowship and commiseration. I needed their testimonies— for hope and unity and reassurance of my own sanity. I needed to find the people who understood the ways clinical anxiety bleeds through to religion and spirituality.

In my search bar, I added the word "Christian" to "Generalized Anxiety Disorder." It yielded practices of local Christian therapists. I already had a therapist. So I deleted "Christian" and tried "Jesus." More Christian therapists, plus some books and articles about worrying less and trusting God more. So I widened my topic to "religion" instead of "Christianity." Then I tried "God." And still, nothing. I reduced "Generalized Anxiety Disorder" to "anxiety disorder," and then to plain old "anxiety." As my search terms widened, more articles and organizations and Christian leaders and writers emerged.

But they only reminded me of Truths I'd been absorbing for years:

"God takes care of the sparrows and the lilies... how much more does He care for you!"[1]

"When you're anxious, pray, give it to God, and the peace of God, 'which surpasses all understanding will guard your hearts and minds in Christ Jesus.'"[2]

"Let go, and let God."

My hopes fell as each URL offered the same exact perspective as the previous. Each article and blog was founded on the premise that anxiety and depression are solely spiritual struggles to be resolved through solely spiritual Truths and practices. "Revise your theology," essentially, was my cure.

I get it: the Bible drips with rich Truth about the faithfulness of God, and there is much to say on the topic. The more we are able to trust Him, the less there is to worry about. It is one of the most important concepts for us to grasp in our Christian lives. Seemingly endless books on the subject have helped millions of people mature their faith in God and overcome everyday anxieties and fears that all people encounter.

But.

The Truths—the ones on which pastors and writers expounded and reflected and applied—were not new to me. I had the great privilege of being raised in them. You will find them all throughout this book. In fact, it is God's nearness and faithfulness that has sustained me throughout this entire journey.

As life-changing as books on spiritual anxiety can be, their content and approach are entirely different from what believers with clinical anxiety need. What we need is complex and nuanced: We need permission to *not* overcome. We need acknowledgment that anxiety disorders are thorns like Paul's, not spiritual deficiencies. We need our faith family to "be quick to listen and slow to speak."[3]

That night back in 2007 left me staring into my laptop's glowing screen in disbelief. According to the Church's silence, I was alone, the only Christian experiencing the kind of crippling anxiety that devotionals weren't mentioning.

Anxious with Jesus was conceived that night 18 years ago because what Toni Morrison said is true: "If there's a book that you want to read, but it hasn't been written yet, then you must write it." And so I hope and pray that this book helps you find the fellowship, understanding, and guidance that I longed to find that night, and most of all, I hope it points you to the presence of Jesus through it all.

PART one

The only one that's never left me

Has carried me so very far

I've heard it said that He wastes nothing,

So beautiful to behold

The author of my hope is writing

The greatest story ever told

REESE ROPER *"THE GREATEST STORY EVER TOLD"*
// FIVE IRON FRENZY

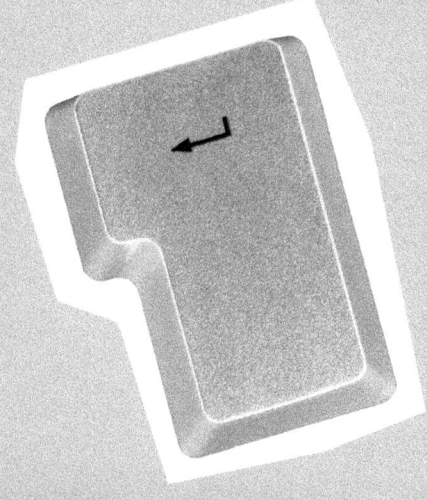

Beginnings

Chapter 1: Early Years

When I met my first computer in 1989, it made me cry. It was an Apple IIE, and I was a curly-haired Kindergartner staring into its glowing green screen. A handful of other kids sat nearby, and a new-to-me teacher hovered behind us as she delivered instructions to our little after-school enrichment group:

"Press 'E'... press 'A'... press 'T'."

One at a time, I found the keys. Success.

Then she said, "Press RETURN."

My tiny muscles tensed and some panic juice dripped into my bloodstream.

WHAT DOES THAT MEAN? WHAT IS "RETURN"?!

Then more letters: "Press 'F'... 'O'... 'O'... 'D'."

But I was frozen, stuck at that mysterious word.

She said it again: "Press 'RETURN'."

I looked at the other kids. No one else looked panicked. I was the only failure.

Utterly lost, and too shy to ask for help, I burst into hysterical tears and never returned.

Get it? *Returned?*

Here's another Kindergarten story.

It was story time. My classmates and I were sitting criss-cross-applesauce on carpet squares as our young, kind teacher, Mrs. Tagg, read to us from *If You Give a Mouse a Cookie*. Suddenly, I realized I had to pee. But I was too shy to raise my hand and ask to use the bathroom in front of everyone. So, I peed my pants.

That same year, I took my first ballet class. Skipping was involved, and I wasn't very good at it, so my Grandpa Raine practiced with me. We must have been horribly cute. Unfortunately, cute didn't cut it. At the next class, when it was my turn to skip across the dance studio, I sensed myself failing, and at the finish line, I burst into tears. My mom embraced me with a hug and reassurance. Long story short, I never got into Juilliard. That was around the time I also stopped hugging my beloved Grandma Gloria, which made no sense, either.

My teachers and parents took note of my abnormal breakdowns and sudden shyness. My parents talked to my pediatrician, who led us to a child psychologist. I remember playing with dolls in a fake-mirror-room as I answered a woman's questions. In the end, the psychologist had no explanation to offer my parents for my change in behavior; she found no trauma, no abuse, and no diagnosis.

She did offer something, though: she invited me to join an experimental playgroup where overly-shy kids were combined with overly-aggressive kids in hopes that they might rub off on each other. My parents hesitated to sign-off on it because who wants to toss their docile fish into a tank of piranhas? But the specialists reassured them. I passed my time as a hair stylist for plastic playdough people and as a chef in a luxurious pretend kitchen. I'm pretty sure most of my playtime was solo, and I'm not sure if it helped much. I wasn't a very self-aware six-year-old. I didn't get beat up by any aggressive toddler gangs though, so I guess it was a pretty good time.

That was the late 80's. Researchers had not yet discovered that "extreme shyness in childhood is one of the strongest predictors of the later development of anxiety disorders,"[1] nor did they know that "children with GAD may appear to be perfectionists"[2] when it comes to things like typing and skipping.

A couple years went by without any core memories weird enough to share here. In fact, childhood was mostly happy times: I aced spelling tests, went to birthday parties, and flipped a lot of Pogs with my sister, Joanna, two years younger than me, and my brother, David, two years younger than Joanna.

My dad's successful career in HR allowed my mom to stay home and take care of the three of us. She sliced watermelon while we swam in our backyard pool, picked up Hawiian pizza and Crazy Bread from Little Caesars while we played Sega Genesis, and folded our laundry upstairs while we rollerbladed through our safe suburban neighborhood. Our dad treated us to Blockbuster Video on Friday nights, bike rides on Saturday mornings, and Baskin Robbins just before it closed on weeknights when homework was light.

We also went to church. My mom grew up Baptist and met Jesus through Billy Graham on TV one night when I was really little. My dad grew up Presbyterian and encountered God one afternoon as he rounded a curvy freeway in his Chevy Nova. A front tire suddenly blew out—he jumped the median without touching it, landed in oncoming traffic, and then drove on to his college campus with a slightly bent frame, no injuries, and faith in divine protection.

So on Sundays, my parents, siblings and I squeezed into my mom's Buick Century, which she dubbed the "Blue Limo," and headed to Oak Hills Church, a large Evangelical church a mile from our house. At Sunday School, I was entertained by feltboard Bible stories, earned orange Tic-Tacs for answering questions, and feasted on red punch and Goldfish from paper cups that nice church ladies handed out.

During the summers, we went to Vacation Bible School at Oak Hills. One summer day in third grade, after crafts, relay races, and songs, our leader told us about how Jesus died on the cross for our sins. Then she asked, "Who wants to say 'yes' to Jesus and go to heaven?" Hands went up, and mine was one of them.

"Oh, great! I'm going to say a prayer. If you want to accept Jesus into your heart, then repeat after me: Jesus, thank you for dying on the cross for my sins... so that I can have a relationship with God forever... I love you and I want to follow you with my life.... Amen."

I prayed that prayer along with her. Then life continued as usual.

HELLO, HEALTH ANXIETY.

The first time I told my parents I was dying, I was in fourth grade.

It all started one spring day when my dad called David, Joanna, and I into the computer room. He announced, "This summer, Grandpa and Grandma Schulz are taking a roadtrip to Utah, and one of you will get to go with them! Who wants to go?"

"I do!" we all resounded.

"Okay, then! Unfortunately, they can only bring one of you, so to be fair, we're going to have a coin-toss. The winner gets to go on the trip."

After a series of flips and calls, I was crowned champion. A few weeks later, I buckled-up in the backseat of my grandparents' white Cadillac and left the suburbs of the San Francisco Bay Area for my Grandma Gloria's hometown in Utah. Along the way, we toured the state capitol, laughed at Grandpa Schulz's wild stories about the killer tomatoes of "Sacratomato," won stuffed animals at Circus Circus in Reno, and stretched our legs on mountain trails.

Thanks to an audiocassette tape my grandpa recorded, I also did a lot of math. His voice quizzed me from the car stereo: "Three fours... Five twos... Six eights..."

In the brief pauses, I answered: "12... 10... umm... 48!" I won a nickel for each correct answer. Thanks to countless flashcard sessions with my dad, I came out a billionaire.

When we arrived at Grandma Gloria's sister's house in Utah, I played with a new-to-me cousin, enjoyed home-cooked meals, board games, and a national park. It was all great fun until one night, on our way back to California, I diagnosed myself with cancer in a Best Western bathroom.

I had no need for a doctor or lab work: the evidence was undeniable. I held it between my fingers as I squinted at my horrifying discovery: *split ends!* Except I didn't know about split ends, and so my mind raced to the panicked conviction that *this must be cancer!* It was simply too bizarre to be anything else. Unprepared to take-on chemotherapy or ruin my grandparents' vacation, I kept my horrifying secret to myself until we arrived home a couple days later.

Knowing full-well that my news would open the darkest chapter of my parents' lives and the final one of mine, I stalled for a few nervous hours. Then I tip-toed into the kitchen where Mom and Dad were going through mail.

"Mom? Dad?"

They looked up from their bills and letters. Warmly, my mom asked, "What is it, Tiffany?"

"There's something wrong with me... Look..."

Solemnly, I showed them my split-ends and burst into tears. I don't remember what they said, but I imagine it must have been hard not to laugh. They pulled me in for a hug and reassured me that I would be okay.

That scene repeated itself a year later. Instead of split-ends though, it was a soft, rubbery lump that protruded from my shin when I squatted. The instant I noticed it, I *knew* it was a tumor. I panicked. Once again, my life was about to be upended, and in turn, I would upend the lives of my family. I said goodbye to our amusement park family vacations. So-long, soccer. No more after-school trips to the Hello Kitty store. Through cancer, I would ruin everything.

An ominous cloud, purple like a bruise, suddenly overshadowed all aspects of life. It covered everyone and everything I loved and cast us all into a nightmare of creepy medical procedures and metal hospital beds and beeping machines and bloody surgeries and bone saws and sketchy chemicals and long needles. I cringed at the thought of my parents watching me go through all of that, all the heartbreak I would drag them through.

To buy us a few more hours of normalcy, I paced around the house in my secret grief, tried to do some homework, and then gave in to my melting emotional state. When daylight dimmed, I wandered through my parents' open bedroom door where my dad was reading. I took a deep breath and unleashed the scary words: "Dad... I found this bump on my leg." My eyes started watering. When the words, "I think it's a tumor," finally fell from my mouth, the tears streamed.

"Kiddo, no, that's crazy!" He put his book down and walked toward me. "Do you know what the odds of that would be?!?"

I looked at him and managed to say, "*WAAAAH-gasp-waaaah-gasp-snottychoke!*"

"Kiddo, I assure you, it's not a tumor... Where is it? Let me look." I squatted so the lump would pop out, and I felt the terrible thing with my fingertips. Then he took a turn. "Kiddo, no, that's not a tumor."

Between sobs, I asked, "Then what is it????"

"I don't know—it's probably a bruise! Or an ingrown muscle! I have one like it in my arm!"

"*WAA*—wait, really?"

"YES! Look! Mine's on my arm right here!" I inspected his arm and touched the bump. "See? I'm fine! *You're* fine!"

His evidence was hard to refute, since he had a bump like mine and wasn't dead and all. He held me until I calmed down and said he wished I wouldn't freak out so much.

But over the years, I kept freaking out.

Like in sixth grade, while brushing my hair, I noticed the little bald spot behind each of my ears. TV taught me that baldness equals cancer, so I took the hint that I was joining the club. Once again, I carried the weight of telling my parents I was dying, and once again, they reassured me that I wasn't.

Later that year, I was trying to fall asleep when I noticed my heart beating. It was just beating, but it felt harder than usual. I was thoroughly disturbed to see my stomach twitch slightly to its rhythm. Nervously, I tiptoed into my parents' bedroom and woke them up so they could take me to the ER because—obviously—I was having a heart attack.

They did their best to convince me it meant nothing, that there are a million reasons for a strong heartbeat. My dad said, "Oooh, kiddo, our hearts have done all sorts of crazy things before, and we're fine!" My mom nodded in agreement. Then he added, "Kiddo, think about all the times you've freaked out like this, and it's always been nothing. You've always been fine. This is another one of those times."

That helped a little bit. I wandered back to bed and began wondering—just a tiny bit—whether my emotions were trustworthy indicators of reality.

It wasn't enough to stop the scary thoughts, though. In the winter of eighth grade, I had nightly headaches. So, brain tumor, obviously.

Back in the 90's when I was constantly dying, health anxiety like mine was called "hypochondria." While my parents realized it was unusual, mental illness simply wasn't on people's radars back then like it is today. In fact, children couldn't even be diagnosed with GAD until 1994.[3] Now, we know a lot more. We know that children with GAD "have catastrophic thinking in anticipation of the worst-case scenario in a variety of situations,"[4] like destroying their families' lives with split ends.

HOLEY MORNINGS

One Sunday morning in eighth grade, in the midst of my health anxiety years, I laid on my pink bedroom carpet, staring up at my popcorn ceiling, fully dressed for church in a magenta romper, chunky black heels, and colorful socks. I was dreading junior high youth group and contemplating defiance.

My mom interrupted my brooding: "TIFFANY HURRY UP AND FINISH GETTING READY FOR CHURCH!"

"BUT I DON'T *WANT* TO GO TO CHURCH!!!" As I said it, I kangaroo-kicked my platform heels through my flowery wallpaper and into the drywall. I don't remember what followed, but it's safe to say that I ended up at church that morning.

The thing about junior high youth group at Oak Hills Church was that it was junior high. But also, unlike the popular kids, I didn't like the social games that monopolized our time. I liked hearing about Jesus, but that part seemed to have a five minute cap. I felt awkward and mostly unseen. Thank God, I had a couple friends who related. With them, youth group was bearable, but without them, it was a thing to be dreaded.

I served my time in junior high until one morning, on "promotion Sunday," I was released. My graduating eighth grade class was led from the converted minister housing where we met, across a sprawling parking lot, past the sanctuary where "big church" met, to the youth chapel where the high school group met on Sunday mornings and Thursday nights.

A sea of high schoolers wearing baggy jeans, puka shell necklaces, and all things Roxy and Stussy spilled out of the chapel's open doors onto a central lawn where they socialized as the last generation to enjoy an adolescence free of smartphones and social media. Inside the chapel, the grass thinned out into an old, green carpet. Maroon chairs sprouted in widespread rows. On a humble stage, also carpeted in green, a drum set, electric guitar, bass, and amp awaited their players.

As I walked toward the entrance, a couple of pretty, bubbly upperclassmen approached me. "Hi, I'm Lisa! And this is my friend, Amanda! What's your name?"

"Hi, I'm Tiffany."

"Nice to meet you, Tiffany! Are you one of the new freshmen?"

"Yah."

"Cool. We're both juniors at Las Llamas. What school are you going to?"

"Fern High."

"Cool!"

"Do you play any sports?"

And it went on like that until, inside, the band started playing "Lord I Lift Your Name On High." Students funneled through the doors and into the seats. Thankfully, I landed next to one of my middle school friends. With the exception of the bass player, the band members all looked like students, and in the audience, nearly everyone clapped along and appeared to actually mean what they sang. I was impressed. This was a new thing.

A goofy icebreaker followed the music, and then a middle-aged, mustached man named Greg stepped onto the stage. He had a gentle spirit and 20 years of experience pastoring teens at Harvest. (All 90's youth groups had vaguely Biblical names like "Harvest.") Greg was devoted to Jesus, prayer, his family, missions, and us. His talks evoked laughter, reflection, and discussion. He helped us realize Jesus's deep love for us and the relevance of the Gospel to our teenage lives.

The following Sunday, as I was walking toward the youth chapel at Oak Hills, the same bubbly upperclassmen crossed my path. Their simple words weighed heavily on the trajectory of my life:

"Hi, Tiffany! We're glad you're here!"

They remembered my name! They're happy to see me!

And just like that, I belonged.

After a few good Sundays, I found the curiosity and courage to show up to a Thursday night gathering. I stepped from my mom's Blue Limo into the twilight of some hundred rambunctious teenagers laughing, playing, and flirting in front of the chapel. The program soon started with a couple ridiculous games—something like chubby bunny, bobbing for goldfish, or shuffle your buns. Then Greg got up and delivered a message that invited us into the depths of Jesus's unconditional love. Afterward, we split into small groups and shared our real struggles and experienced authentic fellowship. The Gospel was preached to us where we were, and it was modeled by our pastor and his team of volunteer leaders. The love of God was there, and week after week, it drew me in.

Harvest quickly became a home where I lived out my high school years. I made new best friends there and before long, I was picking up my school besties in the Blue Limo to join us. We bonded on snowboarding trips, weekend retreats, and annual week-long mission trips to Mexico.

In the meantime, my home life erupted into a bit of chaos when my sister was hit with a mental health struggle of her own. That's another story for another book, maybe. I'm telling you that much now, though, because "Good timber does not grow with ease; the stronger the wind, the stronger the trees."[5] When my family was unstable, God was growing a root system within my soul grounded in Him.

In the summer after my junior year, Greg took a group of us upperclassmen to the Czech Republic where we helped a small village rebuild a church that the former communist government destroyed. We spent early mornings having devotions alongside a babbling creek before walking to the work site where we pic-axed, shoveled, and wheelbarrowed our way into the afternoon. After lunch, we played with orphans, hiked with locals, and taught conversational English. At night, we feasted on food made by village grandmothers and absorbed eye-opening stories from our new Czech sisters and brothers.

This is all to say that my suburban upbringing wasn't only physically privileged; it was spiritually privileged. I was profoundly shaped by all of it. And I haven't even mentioned what will likely sound like the weirdest part: There was a thriving Christian punk and ska scene in the 90's, both nationally and locally. My friends and I moshed on weekends, and bands like Five Iron Frenzy and the Supertones became deeply influential in the formation of my identity and faith.

Unfortunately, my maturing faith didn't have much of an affect on my health anxiety. A few weeks after returning from the Czech Republic, I hopped on another plane—this time to Hawaii with my family. One night, at a luau, my hands started tingling. I paced nervously through the tropical darkness because everything was about to change, again. I had diabetes, obviously. And this time, I was crushed under an extra burden of guilt: *If only I had lost some weight, then I wouldn't have ruined my parents' lives with this disease.* Per my usual MO, I kept my awful news a secret so as not to ruin vacation (and life) for everyone else.

When we returned to the mainland, I shared my awful secret with my parents. They made an appointment for me with our family physician, Dr. Lee, whom I had known since I was 10 years old. He is an affable, middle-aged, Asian American man always dressed in a white collared shirt, black slacks, and a stethoscope.

On the day of my appointment, he greeted me with an enthusiastic, "Hi! How are you? What's been going on?"

From the exam table, I nervously answered, "I'm okay, but I've been having some tingling in my hands." A pause. "I'm afraid it's diabetes."

He gave me a knowing smile that said, *I highly doubt that.*

After a brief exam, he said, "I know what's going on—you're hyperventilating!"

"What?!" I raised my eyebrows. Hyperventilation was for people at marathon finishing lines and swim clubs after nearly drowning. It's not for touring Maui.

Seeing my confusion, Dr. Lee elaborated: "It's very slight. You're only taking two or three extra breaths per minute, so you probably don't even notice it."

It couldn't be that simple.

"Here, let me show you!" He opened a cupboard and handed me a paper bag. "Breathe into it fast, like this," he gestured. I did.

Surprised, I exclaimed, "My hands are tingling again!"

"Yes! See? No diabetes! The cause is hyperventilation."

He taught me how to correct it with belly breathing and counting my breaths: Inhale 1-2-3-4, hold 1-2, exhale 1-2-3-4.

Unfortunately, the word "anxiety" didn't come up during that appointment. It wasn't because Dr. Lee was a bad doctor; he is actually a renowned diagnostician. I think he didn't explore anxiety because it was only 2000. Back then, in middle school and high school health classes, we learned about things like peer pressure, drugs, sex, relationships, and STDs, but short of suicide, nothing was mentioned about anxiety or depression. Knowing nothing of intrusive thoughts or suicidal ideation, people commonly believed that suicide was simply selfish. People teased each other with burns like, "You belong in a mental institution!" "You're crazy! Did you forget to take your pills this morning!?"

For most of us, mental illness didn't hit close to home. Or more likely—we didn't *realize* it hit close to home. Whatever the case, the awareness wasn't there. Neither social media, nor smartphones, nor the pandemic had shown up yet to alter adolescence and spread (awareness of) anxiety and depression far and wide. We didn't know that twenty years later, 1 in 8 of us would be taking antidepressants, 1 in 5 would be receiving "some kind of mental health care,"[6] and the surgeon general would declare a mental health crisis among America's youth.[7]

If that appointment with Dr. Lee had occurred in 2025, I'm sure there would have been follow-up questions about other anxiety symptoms, like,

"How's your sleep been?"

"Have you been feeling nervous a lot?"

"Have you been having difficulty concentrating?"

But also, for all I know, maybe Dr. Lee *did* ask those questions, and maybe my answers were,

"Ok."

"No."

"No."

After all, my symptoms didn't hit all at once. Years later, I would learn that this is characteristic of GAD, which "usually has a gradual onset, so people [like me, and even my doctor] may not recognize the symptoms as they build up."[8]

ADOLESCENCE AND ETERNITY

By my late adolescence, my health anxiety began to fade, but something new emerged. Instead of getting stuck on my failure to skip perfectly, use a keyboard, or ruin my parents' lives, my perfectionism settled on people and eternity, which is as fun as it sounds.

Here's an early memory of it. It was my first year of college. I lived on campus at UC Davis, an hour north of my Bay Area hometown. A beautiful thing about dorm life is that you become friends with people you otherwise probably wouldn't. Luke was one of those people. He was an outspoken atheist and I was an on-fire Christian, but because we lived in the same building, because he was dating my friend, and because we both liked punk, we became friends. We debated the existence of God on AIM, and of course, like a faithful believer, I regularly and obnoxiously invited him to Campus Crusade (now "Cru"), the weekly campus fellowship I had joined.

One Thursday morning, he said yes. Later that night, as we walked with my friends to the lecture hall, I felt important things hovering on the horizon. When we got there, an emcee made us laugh, and then a worship band started playing. Most people stood, some sat; some clapped, some didn't. There were choices to make. I got to my feet. Luke didn't. And then eternity suddenly spun off its axis and landed on my shoulders.

OMG I should be sitting down with Luke! He's feeling more alienated and isolated by the second... a brave atheist, drowning alone in a sea of worshiping Christians! If I simply sat with him, like Jesus would have, then he'd feel cared for and seen! Then he'd realize the reality of God's love for him! Then Jesus would meet him here! But instead, I'm derailing his path toward God by standing!

I felt responsible for a spiritual freeway wreck. My heart pounded. My breathing got weird.

Maybe the damage isn't irreparable, I hoped. So I sat down with him like Jesus sat down with his disciples.

But the panic sat down with me and shoved its condemning finger in my face.

If Luke saw me worshiping more passionately, standing, then he'd know my faith was real, and then he'd want it for himself!

But because I sat down, all he's seeing is a phony, and now he extra-believes that religious people are all phonies. (Shoutout to Holden Caulfield!)

When the worship songs ended, my obsessing didn't. I felt like some evil magician who made Luke's seed of faith disappear into thin air. And when the night's speaker wrapped up their message, I was still stuck in fight or flight.

That night, like so many other times, my thoughts were accompanied by emotions so strong that I never questioned their validity. I didn't know brains could be usurped so subtly. I didn't know my thoughts needed to be worked through. I didn't know there were names for the kinds of intrusive thought patterns I was dealing with—names like "catastrophizing" "mind reading," and "all-or-nothing thinking."

I didn't even know that the word "anxiety" applied to my life at all. I thought "anxiety" was simply worry that results from a failure to fully trust God and submit my will to His. It turns out that a lot of the time, "anxiety" does mean that. But not always. There is another kind. A kind that I would soon be told did not exist.

Chapter 2: Onset: When I Didn't Feel Like Me

In June of 2002, at Oak Hills Church, I sat through the most memorable sermon I've ever heard. My high school friends and I had just returned from our first year of college. I had spent several weekends at home that year, which meant Sunday mornings at Oak Hills Church without my beloved Harvest youth group. In its place, I had been attending the main adult service at 9am, followed by the college and career group, "Refine," at 11am.

So on the morning of that most memorable sermon, I thought I knew what to expect—I knew that the music would be too tame and adult-contemporary for my taste, and I knew that the sermon probably wouldn't evoke much emotion, either. But I also knew that God was beyond all of that. I think showing up is an act of faith that God delights in. He meets us in the Truth, and I knew Truth was spoken and sung there. Plus, I was excited to see my old friends from Harvest who had been away at college. To be with them was to be at Church.

The difference between my experience at Oak Hills before and after my high school years at Harvest is hard to explain. I mean, sure, church services don't offer the fun and games of youth group, and I know that glory days come and go. I wish I had a succinct and fair way to explain it, but this will have to do: I think something important—like authenticity or humility or vulnerability—got lost in Oak Hill's larger quest for precision—a precise doctrine, precise instructions for Christian-living, precise handshakes and precise smiles. Unlike the Gospel-centered talks given at Harvest, the sermons at "big church" expounded on everything a Christian should know, should do, should say, and should believe. This included which aspects of mainstream culture Christians should avoid: things like *The DaVinci Code*, *Harry Potter*, and as I was about to find out—therapy and the psychiatric medication that sometimes accompanies it.

And so on that warm June morning, I sat in the sanctuary next to a few old friends from Harvest and a bunch of new acquaintances from Refine. Everyone was speaking in politely hushed tones until a short, stout worship pastor stepped into the spotlight. His radio-announcer voice resounded from the speakers: "Rise, let us stand and worship the Lord!" He raised his extended arms like a conductor, and like his musicians, we rose to our feet. A sea of designer blouses, pressed blazers, and smooth, shiny hair rose in front of me. I was wearing my usual jeans, frizzy ponytail, and a band t-shirt from the previous night's punk show. We sang, and the songs passed like tracks on a CD, until the pastor-conductor announced to us, "You may be seated."

Then another man, Pastor Calihan, approached the polished pulpit. He was about my parents' age, clean-shaven, and always in a suit. He had been the head pastor of Oak Hills Church for as long as I can remember. In his typical paternal tone, he introduced his sermon: "Today, we are continuing our series entitled 'Sola Scriptura.' 'Sola Scriptura' is a Latin phrase coined by Martin Luther back in 1584, meaning 'only scripture.'" He explained that Christians are called to rely on scripture alone to live joyful, God-pleasing lives in Christ, and for proof, he read from 2 Timothy 3:16-17:

> All scripture is God-breathed and beneficial for teaching, for rebuke, for correction, for training in righteousness; so that the man of God may be fully capable, equipped for every good work.

His exposition of the text continued as it would on any Sunday, and I wouldn't remember that day at all if it weren't for his next words. They bulked up, bounced off the sanctuary's towering walls, and struck me in the gut:

"Scripture is the only weapon needed by the faithful believer to win the fight against depression and anxiety! Believers need not look to worldly sources like secular therapy and medication! Anxiety and depression are spiritual ailments that need spiritual remedy! Scripture alone is enough, and if it isn't, then you need more faith!"

He explained that anxiety is a failure to trust God with our present and future. He cited the words of Jesus Himself: "Do not worry about tomorrow, for tomorrow will worry about itself."[1] And then the words of Paul:

> Do not be anxious about anything, but in every situation, by prayer and petition, with thanksgiving, present your requests to God. And the peace of God, which transcends all understanding, will guard your hearts and your minds in Christ Jesus.[2]

"Therefore," he concluded, "anxiety results when we fail to pray with enough faith, or with a pure-enough heart, or when we don't submit ourselves fully to God. Depression is actually selfishness in disguise, because instead of 'fixing our eyes on Jesus Christ,' we're fixing our eyes on ourselves and indulging in self-pity!"[3] He reminded us that scripture also says to "Rejoice in the Lord always!" and contrasted that with wallowing in our own sorrow.[4]

"Both anxiety and depression," he concluded, "are spiritual issues, sin issues. Immature faith issues. And the antidotes to those must therefore also be spiritual: Biblical counseling, maturing one's faith, devoting oneself to prayer, and internalizing the Word."

At that point, I stole a glance toward the other twenty-somethings in my row. *Did anyone else feel the gut-punch?* I couldn't help but cringe.

What about people who grew up in abusive homes? What about child soldiers? Tortured POWs? Parents who survive their children? What about refugees? What about the traumatized? What about my little sister? Can't life get so ugly that our brains just fizzle out a bit? Isn't it possible to break and not bend, and not be at fault?

The tragic irony of not only that morning, but of that entire summer, is that I was unknowingly suffering from the very thing that Pastor Calihan so grossly misunderstood and misspoke of. Because my symptoms didn't match the church's description of "anxiety," I was clueless that I was experiencing the clinical version of it, the one I was just taught did not exist.

THAT ONE SUMMER

Just a week before sitting through that sermon, I was in Albania, on yet another mission trip, with a small team of fellow college students and retirees from Oak Hills Church. Somewhere between teaching English classes and serving alongside our sister church, something started going horribly wrong in my chest. My heart started skipping beats and pounding double-hard on others. It felt like some tiny, unwelcome DJ was hosting a weeklong rave in my ribcage.

I was pretty sure I was dying, but I kept it from my team like I kept my hair cancer from my grandparents a decade earlier. When I got home from our two-week trip, I soberly delivered my "I'm dying" speech to my parents. I was 19, but there were still hysterical tears. They assured me it was nothing, but said I should go to see Dr. Lee just in case.

On the day of my appointment, I sat in the waiting room, thumbing through magazine pages to distract myself from my impending doom. I tried not to, but I couldn't help imagining the words "heart disease" in my doctor's voice. I envisioned the operating table I'd eventually lay on and the incredible force required to crack my ribcage open.

I worried for myself a little bit, but mostly, I couldn't bear the thought of leading my family into the nightmarish world of bloody scalpels and machines that pump yellow liquids through rubbery flesh.

"Tiffany?"

The nurse led me from my dark imagination to a familiar exam room where I awaited Dr. Lee for sentencing. Sitting on the exam table's crinkly paper, I felt myself morphing into a medical experiment as he appeared and stuck little pads and wires all over my chest. A moment later, his machine was printing my results onto some sort of CVS receipt. I held my breath as he examined it.

"Well, this looks okay! It's heart palpitations!"

"Wait, heart *what*!?!? Aren't those *bad??!!*"

"No, no. They're not a big deal. Here's what I want you to do: Quit caffeine for six months, get more sleep, and relax. Okay?"

"Okay... yes... okay... So no coffee for six months, sleep more, and relax?"

"Yes. What are you doing until school starts?"

"I don't really know yet... um.... I just got back from Albania, and there's not really enough time to find a job or anything, so I'll probably just hang around at home."

"Oh, good! So you can relax, then!"

"Yes, I can do that."

"Great, see me in six months, then."

"Ok." My stiff shoulders melted, and I fully exhaled for the first time in weeks.

Unfortunately, Dr. Lee and I were both wrong. Despite my open schedule, the sunny summer days, and the pool in my parents' backyard, I couldn't relax, and rejuvenation was out of the question. Something was wrong with me besides my palpitating heart, but it was a peculiar and elusive sort of "something."

It was a cramped, constricted throat. It was tingling fingers, and a new version of breathing: shallower and somehow sharper than usual. Several times a day, some mysterious chemical burst in my throat and seeped into my chest with a cold burn. I couldn't make sense of it—I didn't feel sick—I just felt *off*, and I didn't have words to describe my symptoms. I just didn't feel like me.

GOD'S GENERALIZED FAILURE

Worse than my physical anomalies was the shift in my thoughts and emotions. I was on edge constantly. Jumpy. Restless. My thoughts were disjointed. I was unable to concentrate.

What I remember of that summer between my freshman and sophomore year of college is not the events, but the feelings. I remember my nervousness as I paced across my parents' squishy living room carpet. I remember the sleek black shine of my sister's grand piano[5] as I puzzled at my new state of being. I remember the cold tightness in my chest as my mom and I glided along the freeway to Ikea. I remember my heart pounding as I tried to convince myself that God wasn't utterly disappointed in me for redecorating my bedroom instead of spreading the Gospel. I felt like I was failing my savior and derailing eternity for the sake of a duvet cover and curtains.

Worst of all though, my communion with God changed. I was used to a rich prayer life. I was used to staring at stars while communing with their Creator. I was used to reading scripture and journaling daily, and all of it came fairly naturally.

Although my spiritual practices and devotion remained the same, my emotional distance and inability to focus were perplexing. My prayer life dwindled to minutes of forced formalities. Focus, which had always been a natural strength, was suddenly far beyond my reach. I couldn't meditate on scripture like I used to, and I couldn't make sense of the change. *Why did I feel so far from God? Why so hard to connect?*

Knowing nothing of anxiety disorders, I arrived at the only logical conclusion I was offered: *My new state of being must be what "feeling convicted of sin" actually feels like.* I'd heard guys from Refine use that phrase to make vague confessions of sin during prayer request time.

Perhaps, that's what I'm feeling, I reasoned. *If sin distances people from God, and I'm further, foggier, and more absent than ever, then my problem must be spiritual.*

Desperate to get right with God, I searched my soul hard to dig up that deeply-rooted sin, whatever it might be. The good news, I figured, was that repentance would return everything back to normal. I just had to figure out what I needed to repent *of*.

So, I went to all the church things. Persistently, I prayed, I read, I journaled, I cried out, I listened. I submitted to God. But weeks passed by, and I was still coming up empty. The state of peace in which I once lived was gone.

For lack of a well-defined sin to repent of, I started to feel like God's generalized failure. I felt guilty constantly. Because I'd heard respected Christians say that "God gives us peace when we're following His will" (note the lack of scripture reference), I figured that I must be failing a lot. I second-guessed my every move. The divine voice I once felt say, "You're my daughter who is incredibly loved," had somehow morphed into, "You're a failure who is ruining eternity."

Instead of knowing God as my loving, powerful, compassionate Father, He became a stereotypical 1950's father: cold, distant, and hunkered down behind an impenetrable Sunday newspaper. All I really wanted was His approval. I wanted Him to peer over His sports page and watch me do a somersault. I wanted to feel Him smile at my attempt to make Him proud. But my exhausting efforts only got me muffled sighs and tight-lipped nods of disapproval. I kept letting Him down. He'd retreat behind His newspaper again. Distant. Impossible to please. But not His fault—mine. I was quite a disappointment to my beloved Father. I had become, in some whack abyss of my mind—His little failure.

Longing to live in His peace like I used to, I sought out "eternally meaningful work." You know, the obvious stuff like serving others and saving souls. Since it was still summer, I looked to that college and career group, Refine, for opportunities. But rather than finding ways to serve our community and share the Gospel like I did in Albania, I found a lot of awkward social gatherings labeled as "fellowship events."

The gender roles were so confined: the "ladies" gathered one Saturday afternoon to bake cookies for the guys, and when the folding chairs needed moving, it was always the "gentlemen" who were beckoned. This was awkward for me because I'm more of a chair-folder than a Saturday afternoon baker. The ladies were taught to softly live out Proverbs 31, and it was the gentlemen's job to choose a young woman to pursue and lead into marriage. I felt like I was trapped in an awkward dating corral that I didn't belong in. All questions of theology and psychology had black-and-white answers. Coloring in the lines was all the rage, and it was hard being me because I'm more into gray scribbles.

I can't be too hard on that group, though. That summer, it probably would have been impossible for me to feel at home anywhere. Sure, Refine had its issues, but so did I. It was my own undiagnosed anxiety disorder that left me isolated and socially dysfunctional. Before that summer, I was the bubbly, hyper, empathetic girl who loved spontaneous adventures and connecting with people. But that summer, I wasn't that person.

One Sunday after church, for example, I met up with a group of 15 or so from Refine at a Japanese festival. I spent the entire afternoon obsessing over what I was *supposed* to do with myself:

What food should I order? And when? What line should I stand in? If I end up in the right line, then I'll eat with the right people, and we'll experience deep fellowship. We'll end up serving God together, and He'll be pleased with me again.

I ended up with a Teriyaki bowl, hovering awkwardly around my peers who had ordered the same. My thoughts spun out:

I shouldn't have ordered when I did. Now I'm stuck eating with the wrong people. If I would have just waited, then I'd be eating with the right people and we'd become close and God would use me in their lives and we'd share the Gospel with others. But because I'm an idiot and ordered my food at the wrong time, I'm stuck eating with these lame people who could care less about others and are obsessed with spiritually perfecting themselves for the sake of pairing off.

I was so on edge. My thoughts kept spinning:

We should be spreading Christ's hope here, but instead we're just huddled together in our "sterile Christian bubble" in the name of fellowship.[6]

I should say something. I should challenge the group like Paul did the early churches. Maybe then, I'd be honoring God. Maybe then, I'd feel like myself. Maybe then, I wouldn't be failing His will.

I ended up doing that—sort of. The following Sunday, after Refine's worship service, I approached the leadership about adding some service or outreach events to the summer calendar. The kind elders explained, "When people want to do service or outreach, they just do it."

I guess I was supposed to pull a Nike and "Just do it," but I was only 19 and didn't have the know-how to recruit a team and start a ministry on my own. A little guidance would have been nice. The lack of it probably had to do with me being a "lady." We weren't supposed to lead anything outside of children's ministry or women's ministry. Unfortunately, I wasn't into either.

Having failed to find or form a team to minister with, I considered venturing out solo:

Should I be evangelizing to strangers? The Apostle Paul did it, so why shouldn't I? Is that what God's trying to tell me to do? Will I feel better then? Will I stop hyperventilating? Will I be able to focus again?

I felt the seconds of eternity ticking by. I thought about the souls melting away because I wasn't acting, because I clearly wasn't following God's will. I thought about Jesus's call to "go into all the world and preach the Good News to everyone."[7]

I frantically questioned, *"Is that what He wants me to do — to go into our affluent downtown and strike up conversations with strangers about God?"*

I was too paralyzed in my anxious state to even try. The guilt lingered. No matter what I did or how I spent my time, I "shoulded" on myself:

I should be making the most of every moment because eternity depends on it.

I should be feeling joyful. I should "rejoice in the Lord always!"[8]

I shouldn't be wasting time redecorating my room. It's just vanity. I should invest my time and energy into things of eternal value — stuff moths won't eat and water won't rust.[9] *I'm such a disappointment. Such a failure to my God.*

At some point and for some reason, God's approval of me became contingent on... well... me, and my 'roided-out purpose-driven life. Deep in my bones, though, I never bought into my newfound economy of legalism. Intellectually, I knew that

God accepted me because, well, Jesus. We are saved by grace alone, not works. Salvation cannot be earned.[10] That's what sets Christianity apart from other religions. But I sure felt that condemnation in my chest, in my lungs, in my palpitating heart, and mostly in the fact that I had no idea why any of it was happening.

When I returned to UC Davis that fall, my mind and body mostly went back to normal, probably because my life there already had a clear structure and purpose. But when I graduated from college and started my career as a teacher, the anxiety came rushing back and nearly drowned me.

Chapter 3: On Sinking and Saving

In my first year of teaching, I was at the end of myself.

The career I'd dreamed of turned out to be a humiliating disaster. Before I was a high school English teacher, in college, I was a popular Young Life leader. I loved the teens I befriended and mentored, and they seemed to love me back. The idea of integrating education and literature into that dynamic made me excited for the future.

When I graduated from my credential program in 2006, I got a job near my hometown and moved back into the house I grew up in. I lived there alone while my parents temporarily lived out of state, which was pretty lonely, especially after living with my best friends for five years. I was eager to dive into my new life as a teacher though, excited to meet my students and create a classroom home for them. I was full of all that romanticized teacher-savior nonsense.

I went from teacher to target within the first few weeks of school. The students I was so excited to serve ignored me, talked over me, and heaved massive attitudes at me, among other things. When I turned around to write on the whiteboard, things went *splat* against the wall: huge spitballs made in the bathroom, clay stolen from ceramics, and balls made of tape from the sports med room. Thank God, I was never hit. It certainly hurt, though.

Between classes, when my teenage bullies spotted me entering the staff bathroom, they'd shove a metal garbage can against the door in some lame attempt to trap me. Thankfully, because students never bothered to throw their trash away, the cans were always light and posed no actual obstacle. Each time it happened, though, it took a toll on my self-esteem, because you know, the more often you're led to self-affiliate with a garbage can, the more you start to... well... self-affiliate with a garbage can. I didn't want my bathroom bullies to know that, though, so I never acknowledged it. I never glared through the throngs of teenage cliques to try to identify my tormentors. I pretended not to notice. I didn't want to give them the satisfaction.

Making the workdays exponentially worse was the fact that a seasoned, tranquil teacher spent her prep period at a desk in the back of the room during my hardest class. She watched kids ignore me, give me attitude, and shout across the room to their friends. She listened to me doing my best to make it stop and help them learn. It was humiliating. She pitied me and tried to help. She said things like, "Don't be scared to send them to the office. Just pick one and send him down. Make an example of him."

I smiled back through my shame, fighting back tears, and responded, "Yah. You're right. Ok." But in my head, I retorted,

But what about everyone else who will protest the "unfairness"? It will be a mutiny! Bad behavior occurs 10 students at a time! How can I choose which one to kick out? And then that kid will tell the administration about how horrible my class is! I'll be found out and exposed as a terrible failure and I'll get pink-slipped and all those years of college will be for nothing! If the administration finds out I'm struggling, it'll all be over!

One day, a kind student stayed after class to let me in on a secret: my students were passing around a petition to get me fired. I shed a couple tears in a bathroom stall that day.

I was doing all I could, but it never seemed to matter. I could write another book about all the factors that contributed to that tumultuous first year of teaching, but here, suffice it to say that it had a fair amount to do with my undiagnosed anxiety disorder. It was stealing my ability to think deeply, be decisive, be myself, and fully function.

After enduring my daily trainwreck at work, I went home to my parents' empty house where I microwaved a sad frozen dinner, packed up my heavy laptop, and forced myself into a coffee shop where I labored anonymously for hours, trudging through data, scouring sources, and scraping together narrative from my classroom-based research. I was working on my Master's degree, which in hindsight seems like awful timing. Back then, though, it felt stupid not to. It was a feature of my credential program—in only two extra quarters, I'd have a Master's in Education.

After my lonely laptop date, I'd drive home in the dark, throw on my pajamas, and because I was so desperate for human connection, watch a couple episodes of *Scrubs* on DVD. The characters reminded me that I wasn't alone. We were all young professionals, straight from grad school, becoming increasingly disillusioned with each workday. I knew their demanding season of loneliness, the longing for connection, the relief in laughing about it, and the glimpses of growth and joy along the way. They helped me through my quarter-life crisis. But because fiction isn't enough, I sometimes opted to wander around Target just to be around non-fictional people. Nights culminated in crying myself to sleep before waking up and doing it all over again. I listened to "Young and Depressed" by MxPx a lot that year.

I was probably listening to it when I was speeding down the freeway on my way home from work one day when I caught a glimpse of Petsmart. It gave me an idea: I could *buy* a companion, like a hamster! After about three seconds, the thought depressed me: How desperate *was* I? Plus, I really didn't have the time or motivation to clean a hamster cage. So I called my dad instead. I ended up confessing, "You know, I'd be fine with it if I happened to die. Like, I'm not saying I *want* to die, but if it was my time, and a car flew over the divider and hit me head on, I'd be okay with it. Like, I wouldn't be missing out on much."

WITHOUT WORDS

Another after-school conversation happened when I ran into Mrs. Gatz while grocery shopping. She is the mom of one of my best friends from Harvest, and I'd known her for nearly a decade. She and her husband were the parents with whom everyone felt comfortable talking—always warm, nurturing, and hospitable. Mrs. Gatz is also Biblical counselor, trained at Oak Hills Church. Conversations with her had always been easy, organic, and colorful. But the day that she spotted me in the produce section and excitedly steered her shopping cart toward mine, it took me a concentrated effort to interact with her. I was probably panicking about whether or not God wanted me to buy strawberries or something. My mind felt like a huge swimming pool, and I was confined to the steps, mentally paralyzed and physically tense. I did my best to engage with her—the conversation itself is a blur—and then we parted ways. She called me later that night.

"Hi, Tiffany! This is Laura Gatz!

"Oh, hi!" I was surprised. While I'd received a zillion calls from her daughter over the years, I'd never gotten one from her.

"How are you?" she asked.

"Hey! I'm doing okay! It's good to hear from you!"

"Hey, when I ran into you at the store today, it seemed like something was wrong... like you were a little 'off,' so I thought I'd give you a call. Are you doing okay?"

I explained my difficult circumstances: how teaching was rough and I was working on my Master's degree and living alone in my parents' big house, which was all hard. I had words for my circumstances, but none for the ineffable mess that had usurped my mind and body.

Before we hung up, she gave me encouraging words and said a prayer for me. I was grateful that she genuinely cared. It ended kind of awkwardly, though. I sensed that Mrs. Gatz hoped I might have more to say. But the truth was that I didn't know how to explain how I felt because *I* didn't understand how I felt. I was so disoriented by the descent of my undiagnosed anxiety.

The sad part is that as a Biblical Counselor, she was unequipped to screen my symptoms. There were no questions about sleep, muscle tension, nausea, concentration—no questions that involved the body. It was a shame, especially because I was suffering from so many of them. That wasn't Mrs. Gatz's fault, though. She didn't fall asleep in her counseling class during the lecture on anxiety disorders. It simply was not included in her Biblical counseling curriculum, which came from a conservative Christian college whose chancellor still fails to acknowledge the realities of mental illness.

SHELTER

I was at a low point, and had nothing to give. Church was no exception. I had no desire to exchange pleasantries, no tolerance for easy Christian platitudes, no patience for straining out gnats.[1] All I had to offer was loads of cynicism. These lyrics to "Secret of the Easy Yoke" by Pedro the Lion hit the spot:

> *I could hear the church bells ringing*
> *They peeled aloud Your praise*
> *The members faces were smiling*
> *With their hands outstretched to shake*
>
> *It's true they did not move me*
> *My heart was hard and tired*
> *Their perfect fire annoyed me*
> *I could not find You anywhere*

My heart *was* hard and tired. At Oak Hills and the many faith communities like it, I felt like a blob of oil floating in a sea of water. I didn't mesh. "My heart was hard and tired," and their hearts—as they presented them, anyway—were confident and cheerful. "Their perfect fire annoyed me" because mine was smoldering out, and I seemed to be the only one.

Thank God for Shelter. I attended their gatherings for a couple years on-and-off when I was home for weekends during my college years. (I stopped attending Oak Hills after my summer with Refine.) Shelter was the epitome of a come-as-you-are church. Some 50 or 100 no-frills people rented a no-frills space where they met on Sunday nights. It was a small community of humble creatives who didn't care for appearances. Vulnerability was valued. Weakness was expected and accepted. One of the pastors there, Justin McRoberts, had recorded a cover of that Pedro the Lion song, "Secret of the Easy Yoke," which was a good sign.[2] Shelter was a place for weak people like me to belong and collapse into the rest of God.

During that first year of teaching, I limped through Shelter's open doors every Sunday night. Sometimes, before service, we'd have a potluck where we welcomed homeless people from the park across the street. The pastor wore flip flops and talked about Jesus a lot. There were no lasers or smoke machines or expectations to give firm handshakes to strangers. Worship looked all kinds of ways: sitting in silence, receiving prayer and a long hug, kneeling on the thin carpet, lighting candles for loved ones, and drawing on butcher paper taped to the wall. It was beautiful and unpretentious and just what a cynical, burnt-out soul like myself needed.

In the midst of my exhaustion and empty hands, God met me there. Sometimes, other people did too. People like Kim, a spunky, kind brunette my age whose Southern accent slipped out every now and then. She worked with Capernaum, a branch of Young Life for teens and young adults with special needs. She has a raw sense of humor, and like most people in that church community, she also has a healthy awareness of her dependence on Jesus.

After the sermon one evening, we ran into each other while washing our hands in the bathroom.

"Hey, Tiffany!"

"Hi!"

"Hey, I wanted to ask you something! Bridget, Jess, and I are going to start a book club on Monday nights, and we were wondering if you'd want to join us!"

"Yes! That would be amazing!"

"Okay, cool! I'll let them know and add you to our text group!"

What Kim really did that night was throw me a life preserver. I don't know what I would have done without Monday nights at Starbucks with Kim, Bridget, and Jess. They are all authentic, wild, and free. When I was with them, I became wild and free, too. We were obnoxiously loud, laughed more than we discussed the book (we never even finished it), and we didn't care.

My new friends voiced opinions that often go unspoken at church groups: we disagreed with the author, laughed at his cheesy anecdotes, and made fun of the book's ridiculously long title. For all its quirks, God certainly worked through that book, though. It was about trusting Jesus and taking chances, and it came with discussion questions, which prompted us to talk about real things.[3] Because vulnerability is contagious, their honest responses gave me permission to express my own. It was freeing to be real about how awful my life felt. Around Valentine's Day, I told them I wasn't wearing heart jewelry because I didn't feel much love. They not only understood, but appreciated the integrity of the thing.

My new friends' authenticity inspired me to speak more authentically. If it weren't for them, I probably would have never shared my apathy toward life and death with my dad. I suspect my confession inspired him to rally prayer for me, because a couple weeks later, I met my husband.

It was a Friday night. Like all my other Fridays that year, it had been a bad one. I didn't want to be alone, so I texted Kim. She was at Patrick and Steve's movie night (whoever they were), and she invited me to come over. Desperate for humans, I went.

I knocked on the door, but nobody answered. I rang the doorbell. Still, nothing. I tried the doorknob. It turned. Hesitantly, I opened the door.

"Hello?"

I poked my head in.

It didn't look like the kind of place where 20-somethings lived. It was a huge two-story house with framed family photos all over the walls. There was antique furniture, breakable knick-knacks, and carpeted stairs.

"Hello?" I asked again, as I stepped inside. Silence. *Whose home am I in?*

Then, faint laughter from above. I added my shoes to the pile at the foot of the stairs and followed the low sound of whatever movie was playing upstairs until I discovered human life.

Kim was the only person I knew among the 10 or so silhouetted figures who sat watching a movie in the dark. I sat down in the only empty chair and caught the end of whatever they had been watching. Because I was late to the movie and lonely, I lingered for a while afterward with Kim, Patrick, and Steve.

The movie room turned out to be Patrick's bedroom, and the house turned out to be his parents'. He and his best friend, Steve, were both renting rooms there. The two of them looked kind of similar, with dark hair and brown skin. They both volunteered on Kim's team of Capernaum leaders. I learned that Patrick worked in IT and Steve was a photographer.

Over the following weeks, I hung out with Patrick and Steve a few more times—in Santa Cruz, at parks, and at restaurants. I texted with Patrick during my depressing coffee shop sessions. Then one night, Steve mysteriously couldn't make it to dinner, and it was just me and Patrick. In the parking lot that night, Patrick asked me out. He felt like home, and we walked into each other's lives.

FRONT ROW SEAT

Like most obnoxious new couples, we hung out... all. the. time. Patrick didn't get the weekly summarized updates on my life that I had to condense for my new book club friends. Rather, he got the full, unabridged saga. He got to know me as the laid-back, bubbly, content person I am. But then he also saw the contrasting anxious version of me: the over-thinking, self-condemning, catastrophizing, on-edge person that anxiety causes me to become.

One night, he stood next to me at Target and watched me obsess over which toothpaste I should buy. As my thoughts spiraled, so did my ability to function. A disaster spun out in my mind:

Ohmygosh which brand am I supposed to get? I suppose God wants me to get the top-shelf toothpaste because He wants me to take care of myself...

But am I more important than His children living in extreme poverty? Who am I to treat myself to the pricey best when they have nothing? God must be frowning down on me for considering indulging my selfish self. I'm such a failure...

So should I buy the cheap generic, then? I'll have more money to support others in need, and He will see my heart and I won't make Him so disappointed...

But then again, Paul "became all things to all men,"[4] and God determined where and when we live.[5] He put me in this affluent suburb, so it must be ok for me to "become" an affluent suburbanite who buys good toothpaste...

But shouldn't I be "in the world, but not of the world"?[6] *And who am I to treat myself when others need clean water?*

It endured horribly. I knew it was stupid, but I couldn't help it. I was embarrassed to be thinking those things, and yet the sheer panic of it all was so real. Patrick saw my tears welling up. I was about to start crying, so we made a bee-line for the car, toothpasteless.

At his church a couple days later, it happened again, except it wasn't toothpaste. After service, everyone was socializing in little groups in the foyer. I was so inexplicably overwhelmed, so uncomfortable, and so tense that I slipped outside into the sunshine. A couple minutes later, he followed me.

"Are you okay, honey?" My eyes watered. "What's wrong?"

He pulled me in for a hug. Tears and hyperventilation filled the silence. He waited patiently.

Finally, between gasps and sobs, I confessed: "I don't know. I don't know what's wrong with me."

He continued holding me. Then softly, he said, "I think you should see someone."

"You mean like professional help? A therapist?"

"Yeah."

"I'm that bad? Like, I can see someone?"

"Yes."

I wasn't offended; I was given permission. Patrick pointed out what I couldn't see. When you're at a low point for a long time, it starts to feel normal. And when a narrative plays so constantly in your mind, it's easy to forget that it might not be entirely true. When change happens subtly over time, it can be hard to notice.

Sometimes we need an outside perspective to point out how we're changing. We need people who are brave and loyal enough to say the awkward things, like "I think you should see someone." We need to let people in closely enough to see the things we'd rather hide, things like tearing up over toothpaste. We need external perspectives to shed light in the dark corners of our souls. It's easier to get lost inside of ourselves than we'd like to think. Isolation is dangerous.

If Patrick didn't say those words, who knows how low I might have plummeted before I got help. One of the hardest things about mental illness is that it isolates us, not only from our fellow humans, but from our very selves. When I can't connect with myself, I can't connect with others, either. And it sucks to be stuck in the darkness alone. It really does.

This is why I needed people like Kim to reach out, and people like Bridget and Jess to take the risk that Kim suggested. They didn't have to invite me into their lives. They were already close friends with each other. They already had deep roots, both inside and outside our little church community. They weren't lonely. They didn't need me.

It was quite the opposite, actually. Inviting me into their group meant taking a risk. They didn't know whether or not I would annoy them, take offense at their edgy jokes, or ruin their dynamic. They could have convinced themselves that I wasn't their responsibility, that it was on me to sign up for fellowship events or approach a welcome center (if we had one), or that it was the responsibility of the staff to get to know me. It's easier to not reach out to disconnected people, the ones who have yet to develop roots in the communities to which we belong. And don't get me wrong, I'm not saying that people on the periphery shouldn't take initiative. We are all called to take steps of faith. But sometimes, we use up all our steps just walking through the door.

Jesus had eyes to truly see the people around Him, and He acted on what He saw. He initiated conversations, asked probing questions, and listened well. He invited all kinds of people into His life who had little to offer: from fishermen to housewives, prostitutes to religious leaders, tax collectors to beggars. He saw their individual needs, and He sees humanity's collective need "to replace our hearts of stone with hearts of flesh."[7] It is that heart of flesh that allows His followers to selflessly seek out people whose needs, by the grace of God, we just might be able to meet. It was through a person God saved the world, and it is through people He continues to save us.

PART TWO

When the concrete of the world
Becomes too cumbersome to lift,
And the cataracts of fear and doubt
Cloak truth beyond what we can sift,
And darkness, darkness bleeds its way,
When crippling anguish clouds our sight—
The ghosts of dusk have bared their teeth,
Set their claws to bring the night—
Hold on,
Hold tight

REESE ROPER *"THESE FRAIL HANDS" // BRAVE SAINT SATURN*

Help

Chapter 4: Diagnosis

A couple days after Patrick gently suggested that I seek help, I called Dr. Lee's office because I didn't know where else to start. The office manager scheduled me for an appointment, and a week later, I was sitting in one of his little exam rooms, listening to his familiar voice through the wall of the adjacent exam room, wondering when the mumbly conversation would fall silent. Minutes later, the silence descended, a door closed, and then a knock on my door before he popped in.

"Hello, there! How are you?" he asked with his usual vim and vigor.

"Hi! I'm doing okay."

"So, what's going on?" He glanced down at the chart in his hands. "You haven't been feeling too well?"

"Yah. Well, I've been having a hard time. I'm not sure what's wrong with me, but I've been really on edge for a while. And my breathing feels weird sometimes—like it's shallow or sharp, if that makes sense. It's hard to describe. And my throat gets sort of tight and constricted. I've been really on edge. It's hard to make decisions and I freak out about things and can't stop even though I know it's stupid. Sometimes, I get overwhelmed and start crying, and I don't even know why. I don't know what's wrong with me."

As he listened, he made a couple notes. Then his eyes widened and he began nodding. "You *have* always been pretty hyper!"

I sensed him connecting the dots between symptoms that were scattered over years and years of medical charts: my heart palpitations, subtle hyperventilation, muscle tension, nervousness.

He lifted his eyebrows and started explaining my prognosis. "So, according to the current research, the most effective way to treat anxiety is something called Cognitive Behavioral Therapy. I'm going to give you the names and phone numbers of three really good Cognitive Behavioral Therapists. I work with all of them, and they are all really excellent. The best ones. I want you to make an appointment with one of them, okay? And then let me know when you do, okay?"

"Yes, I will. Thank you." I nodded in agreement. It was the first time anyone had ever used the word "anxiety" to describe me. I received it just like I received the words "Tonsillitis," "Bronchitis," and "Tuberculosis" over the years (more on that last one shortly).

I was relieved to have next steps. When I got home, I called the only female on Dr. Lee's list, Dr. Wendy Carraway, and left a message.

She returned my call the next day. I didn't know it at the time, but this would prove to be a rarity among therapists. Over the phone, Dr. Carraway's voice was calm, soothing, and confident.

"So, Tiffany, tell me what's going on."

I repeated to her all the things I told Dr. Lee.

She responded, "Okay. Well, it sounds like you might have Generalized Anxiety Disorder. Let's schedule a time for you to come in so we can talk some more." We agreed on next Thursday.

As I hung up, I felt a wave of comfort wash over me. I was relieved that there might be a name for my puzzling state, a diagnosis that could make sense of all the chaos.

When next Thursday rolled around, I drove ten minutes to Dr. Carraway's office. It was downtown in a modest professional building next to a 7-11. I climbed a flight of concrete stairs to her office on the second floor and walked in. I was greeted by a woman of about 50 with a milky complexion, flowy skirt, and a crown of pretty, thick, gray hair.

"Hi, Tiffany, I'm Dr. Carraway, it's so nice to meet you. Come on in."

I sat down on a couch across from her, and as she asked me questions, I told her about everything. And for the first time in a long time, I felt understood.

By the end of that first session, she confirmed my diagnosis: Generalized Anxiety Disorder (GAD). It fit like a glove. The Diagnostic and Statistical Manual of Mental Disorders (DSM) defines it as "excessive anxiety and worry, occurring more days than not for at least six months, about a number of events or activities. The anxiety, worry, or physical symptoms cause significant distress or impairment in social, occupational, or other important areas of functioning."

The worry is difficult to control, and is associated with three (or more) of the following six symptoms:

1. Restlessness or feeling keyed up or on edge (Check.)

2. Being easily fatigued (Check.)

3. Difficulty concentrating or mind going blank (Definitely.)

4. Irritability (That would explain some things.)

5. Muscle tension (We'll get to that in a few pages.)

6. Sleep disturbance (My FitBit says yes.)

CONNECTING DOTS

Equipped with my new diagnosis, I dove deep into the interwebs when I got home. What I found amounted to dots that connected the weirdnesses of my childhood and adolescence.

For starters, I found that "regardless of the age of actual onset, many individuals with GAD report feeling anxious all their lives."[1] That checked out. Anxiety's fingerprints are smeared all over my early years. My late adolescence started to make more sense, too. I learned that when it comes to anxiety disorders, "worries can shift from one concern to another and may change with time and age."[2] That accounted for the transformation of my health anxiety into spiritual perfectionism. After graduating from college, when the anxiety spread to things like grocery shopping and choosing lunch, well, that's when failure to function sent me to Dr. Lee for help.

Even the slow onset of my symptoms and overdue diagnosis made sense, as "rates of missed diagnoses and misdiagnosis of GAD and PD [Panic Disorder] are high, with symptoms often ascribed to physical causes."[3] The timing of my anxiety's full onset makes sense, too, as "life experiences, such as traumatic events [like my first year teaching, apparently], appear to trigger anxiety disorders in people who are already prone to anxiety."[4]

AND MUSCLE TENSION

One thing I haven't told you about yet is my muscles. They're massive. Just kidding. They're tense. Historically, really tense. They were that way long before I knew that "pain can be a common symptom — and sometimes a good indicator — of an anxiety disorder, particularly Generalized Anxiety Disorder."[5] Note that muscle tension is the fifth of six markers of GAD in the DSM. Muscle tension was also the thickest chapter of my medical records.

I won't bore you with all the details. Just some. Like this one: I've been diagnosed with Carpal Tunnel Syndrome (CTS) symptoms three separate times, each during a major life transition when anxiety also blew up (at the end of high school, the end of college, and then a 500 mile relocation to San Diego). While most people associate Carpal Tunnel Syndrome with poor desk ergonomics and repetitive motion, research shows higher rates of anxiety and depressive disorders among people with CTS symptoms than those without.[6] In my case, when I'm stressed, I catch myself tensing my shoulders, upper back, and jaw. That muscle tension interferes with nerves that make my hands tingle and go numb. For this malady, Dr. Lee treated me with hydrocortisone shots in my arms and back, weekly pain massages (my term, not his), bottles of muscle relaxers, and lots of stretching for homework. Each time I had a flare-up, the goal was to avoid surgery, and thankfully, each time, that goal was achieved.

When Dr. Lee was treating me for my second round of CTS, I mentioned a new complaint to him: my jaw clicked from time to time. He handed me a clean urine collection jar to put in my mouth to stretch it out. That didn't help much. He also recommended I talk to my dentist. Unfortunately, at that time, I unknowingly had a bad one.

When I told Dr. BadDentist about my jaw noises, he said, "Oh, yeah! Some people have headaches every day of their lives because of that." The silence that followed spoke volumes of the hope he had for me. At that point, the jaw noises were just a bodily quirk, so I didn't pursue it any further.

A couple years later, however, during that beloved first year of teaching, the clicking exploded into unmanageable pain. My jaw throbbed incessantly. My ears rang. I often considered punching myself in the face because it already hurt that much. I missed work because of it.

When I told a new and improved dentist about it, she referred me to a glorious place called The Center for Orofacial Pain at UC San Francisco. It sounded like it was built just for me. I was so relieved that help existed. I took a day off work and a lot of public transportation to get to my appointment. When I arrived at the medical school campus, lots of questions were asked, measurements were noted, and X-rays were taken. I left with a diagnosis: Temporomandibular Disorder (TMD), a referral to a special physical therapist, prescriptions for Flexeril and Tramadol (which I dubbed my "drunk pills"), a referral for a special two-hour x-ray circuit experience, a follow-up appointment, and an invitation to participate in a study. Eventually, there was an orthodontist, too.

My physical therapist, Arlyn VanDyke, was a friendly, older, Mid-western man and a renowned jaw expert who regularly taught dental students at UCSF about jaw disorders. At first, I saw him twice a week, then once, and until I moved a decade later, I continued seeing him as needed for especially stubborn flare-ups. On a couple occasions, Arlyn mentioned that TMD often comes hand-in-hand with stress, and so he asked if I noticed a correlation: Was I experiencing a lot of stress?

I said "no." It amazes me now that I didn't see it then. Maybe I was in denial. Or maybe I didn't see it because the jaw pain wasn't limited to stressful moments in the classroom: it was chronic and lasted for hours, days, and weeks at a time.

Years into my treatment, Arlyn confessed that he didn't have much hope for me at my initial consultation. Thankfully, God works miracles through the people and science He created. In the end, I learned that my TMD was caused by a variety of factors, including malocclusion (my teeth don't fit together right) and grinding and clenching my teeth in my sleep, which exacerbates everything. And of course, there's that stress I carry in my shoulders and jaw. I have experienced much healing from TMD, but it is a condition I still have to manage from time to time.

NOT EVERYONE'S ANXIETY

GAD can be difficult to understand because while everyone feels anxious from time to time, not everyone has an anxiety *disorder*. It is normal and human to experience anxiety as a product of our fight, flight, or freeze response, which is built into our brains to help us survive life-threatening situations. If confronted by an attacker or chasing down a kidnapper, anxiety releases hormones that make us stronger, faster, and sharper (among other things).

Unfortunately, anxiety also surfaces when we *perceive* danger, regardless of reality. So if I *perceive* that my nosebleed will never stop and land me in an early grave, then anxiety will ensue, which will unfortunately exacerbate the nosebleed. And yes, that is an example from my real life. My six hour nosebleed ended when I walked into the ER.

Disordered anxiety hijacks rational thought at any time, in any place—at the grocery store, at work, during church, in mid-conversation on a coffee date, at a beach during sunset—it has no regard for agendas. It's fight or flight out of context, and it's exhausting. To illustrate the difference between normal and disordered anxiety, I'm going to tell you about my most contradictory day.

It was August. I was 24, recently diagnosed with GAD, and about to start my second year of teaching. For a teacher—especially during those first few years—the week before school starts is a special sort of tornado. I was darting around town in my gray Accord, checking things off my to-do list. My next stop was Dr. Lee's office to get my routine Tuberculosis paperwork signed. At the front desk, I showed him the skin he pricked three days earlier, but instead of signing my form, his eyes got wide. He reached out, felt my arm, and exclaimed, "OH! THAT'S *POSITIVE!*" Immediately, he pulled me back into an exam room, referred me to the hospital across the street for a chest x-ray, and firmly instructed me to "Go, there, *IMMEDIATELY!*"

This is the point at which most people would expect someone with an anxiety disorder to panic, especially if that someone has a history of health anxiety. You'd expect me to be flooded with images of eerily sterile hospital rooms with thick glass windows between my visiting loved ones and myself. You'd expect my imagination to replay period movie scenes of women depressingly hacking up blood into kerchiefs. You'd expect me to be disturbed by the reality of my own mortality and the fragility of everything that had minutes ago felt so rock-solid.

But I didn't think those things. Instead, standing in my paper gown, watching the x-ray technician manipulate her massive machinery, the Holy Spirit reminded me, "In their hearts people plan their course, but the LORD establishes their steps."[7]

I reasoned, *If my x-ray tests positive, there's nothing I can do, so it must be God directing my steps that way for whatever reason. I bet I contracted that rogue TB cell on one of my mission trips to Kazakhstan* (yes, I went there too), *and I have no regrets about any of my summers there.* Jesus said to "take up your cross and follow me."[8] *If TB is part of the cross I have to carry, then okay. If the cost of obedience to Christ is a foreign disease, then that's the cost.*

In that moment of surrender, I was soaking up that "peace that surpasses understanding."[9]

Here's the thing, though. I was so far from peace earlier that morning. I was driving from errand to errand when I had a breakdown at a stoplight. Not an engine breakdown, but a mental one. On the radio, 105.3 was playing Nirvana's "Nevermind." For some reason, I flipped the dial and discovered "Name" by the Goo Goo Dolls on 99.7. And then I felt it: my throat cramped, my breathing changed and my mind revved into crisis mode:

OMG what is the right song to listen to?! Which one will bring me closer to God? If I pick the wrong one, I'll disappoint God and drift even further from Him! So much is riding on this!

"Nevermind" is so fueled with passion. I can feel its Truth reverberating in my heart! But on the other hand, "Name" is about orphans. Its lyrics acknowledge the dignity of the forgotten. Jesus never forgets them.

So I let the dial sit on the Goo Goo Dolls. But the overthinking continued:

Ugh, I chose the wrong song! "Nevermind" has a passion in its sound that is beyond words. I should be listening to that. It will connect me to God's raw passion and the true electricity of life.

So I switched to "Nevermind." But —shocker— my mind kept racing:

What if I don't feel that energy that I thought I would? What if I should be listening to "Name"? I'm ignoring what God says is important—the plight of the orphan and the widow![10] *I am part of the problem. God is so disappointed in me. He's shooting daggers in my direction like Jesus did the Pharisees.*

And back and forth and back and forth it went. I arrived at Dr. Lee's office entirely on edge.

My reactions to the events of that day are clearly inconsistent. Why would anyone be anxious about what to play on the radio and be at peace with a life-threatening illness?! It makes no sense, and yet it makes perfect sense: anyone can get anxious over a TB diagnosis, but only a person with an anxiety disorder can get anxious over which song to play when driving alone.

Chapter 5: What I Learned in Therapy

There's this one time I got stuck in a whirlpool. A literal one. It didn't happen in the ocean, though. It happened in the pine covered hills of Northern California, at a gorgeous Young Life camp property called Woodleaf, in the shallow end of a swimming pool. The whirlpool was the result of dozens of people of all races, backgrounds, and abilities running as one united donut as fast as we could. And when the person who organized the feat yelled, "Legs up!" we floated effortlessly on a speedy underwater merry-go-round. A sassy, short teenager with Down's Syndrome clung to me, piggy-back style, as we laughed throughout the whole thing. It was one of the most joyful moments of my life.

Anxiety is like being stuck in a whirlpool—just not that one. In fact, it's the exact opposite of that one. It's not the fruit of teamwork. It's Goliath grabbing David by the throat. It's not an amusing ride overseen by lifeguards. It's a spinning juggernaut that reduces reality to a blinding blur. It demands 99% of my mental energy just to keep my head above the water. The only thought I can manage is some version of *OH CRAP OH CRAP OH CRAP! HEEELLLLLLP MEEEEE!* And the worst part is—before therapy—I was helpless to escape it.

Thankfully, Jesus showed up to my therapy sessions and brought some special mud with him. He made it in the parking lot by spitting in some dirt. That sentence makes me laugh. It's practically in the Bible, though. His disciple, John, wrote about it:

> "As [Jesus] passed by, he saw a man blind from birth... he spit on the ground and made mud with the saliva. Then he anointed the man's eyes with the mud and said to him, "Go, wash in the pool of Siloam" (which means 'sent'). So he went and washed and came back seeing."[1]

Another disciple, Mark, recorded a similar encounter between Jesus and a blind man in the village of Bethsaida:

> "Some people brought a blind man and begged Jesus to touch him. [Jesus] took the blind man by the hand and led him outside the village. When he had spit on the man's eyes and put his hands on him, Jesus asked, 'Do you see anything?' He looked up and said, 'I see people; they look like trees walking around.' Once more Jesus put his hands on the man's eyes. Then his eyes were opened, his sight was restored, and he saw everything clearly."[2]

Before therapy, my mind's eye was partially blind. Jesus healed my vision much like he did the blind man in Bethsaida—incrementally. In each therapy session, Jesus said, "Close your eyes." Then he gently spread some of his spit on my closed eyes. When my session ended, Jesus said, "Now go, rinse it off." Blindly, I felt my way down the hallway to the bathroom. After splashing some cold water on my face, I opened my eyes to an improved-but-still-fuzzy reality. Later that week, when I inevitably got stuck in an anxiety whirlpool, I was able to discern—for the first time—a rope dangling into the water from above. Over and over, I grasped at it, but my depth perception was still off. I just couldn't get my hands on it. Simply knowing it was there, however, gave me hope.

The following week at therapy, Jesus was there again, and He repeated his ritual. When my hour with Dr. Carraway was up, I washed the mud from my eyes and opened them to greater clarity. The next time I swirled around the anxiety whirlpool, my depth perception was good enough to catch the rope. I clung to it, but my arms eventually fatigued. I floated away with rope burns on my hands. I kept circling, and I kept grabbing the rope, but my muscles were too weak and uncoordinated to hoist myself out. So, Jesus tasked Dr. Carraway with coaching me through strength training. Week by week, my muscle fibers tore and healed, until one day, I finally muscled all the way up that rope and flopped my body onto a shore called Peace. Finally, I soaked in warmth and caught my breath.

I didn't get to stay out of the whirlpool forever, though. Gusts of wind and bullies shoved me back in—but the more times I climbed that rope, the easier it became to escape my cold, wet panic and return to the warm ground of reason.

The training regimen Dr. Carraway used in our sessions was Cognitive Behavioral Therapy (CBT). At first, my workouts focused on relaxation techniques. Then, they were all about cognitive distortions: learning how to identify them, challenge them, and replace them with True thoughts. Gifted psychologists, therapists, and psychiatrists have created all kinds of helpful resources that walk people through the sorts of things I'm about to attempt to explain. I encourage you to look into them. Here, I am simply providing a brief overview of what I personally took from my therapy sessions that I can pass along to you.

RELAXATION TECHNIQUES

The mind and body have a complex, interdependent relationship. Relaxation exercises capitalize on this interconnectedness by controlling things like breathing and muscle tension to positively affect thoughts and emotions. The three main relaxation techniques I learned from Dr. Carraway are diaphragmatic breathing, progressive muscle relaxation, and body scanning.[3]

Breathing Exercises

Dr. Carraway taught me an exercise she called 4-2-7 breathing. It's a type of diaphragmatic breathing, which is just a big word for "belly breathing." In belly breathing, you make your belly, rather than your chest, inflate and deflate like a balloon as you inhale and exhale. To check if you're doing it right, you can put a hand on your belly; if it moves as you breathe deeply, you're doing it right. If it's your chest that's rising and falling, then try again. Belly breathing also involves breathing through your nose and out through your mouth.

To experience relief from stress and anxiety, it is essential to control the rhythm of your breaths. That's what the numbers are for: 4-2-7 means inhaling for a count of four, holding your breath for a count of two, and exhaling for a count of seven (or more). Dr. Carraway told me that the slower the exhale, the better. Pursing your lips can help slow the exhale. That 4-2-7 rhythm is my go-to for deep breathing, but a lot of people prefer other variations, like box breathing, which is 4-4-4. I highly recommend checking out YouTube for some great guided breathing videos to help you get the hang of it.

Muscle Relaxation

Dr. Carraway taught me progressive muscle relaxation (PMR) to help me overcome muscle tension and embrace calm. Basically, it works like this: starting with the toes and progressing up toward the head, tense or flex each muscle group, one at a time, for 5-10 seconds, and then release suddenly. Wait 10-120 seconds, and then move up to the next muscle group (like the calves), and flex them for 5-10 seconds, release, wait 10-20 seconds, and progress to the next muscle group (quads/hamstrings). Continue this until you get all the way up to your eyebrows.

Regularly practicing PMR greatly increased my awareness of muscle tension within my body. I was soon able to do quick body scans to detect and eliminate muscle tension. Body scans are quite similar to PMR, but instead of tensing muscles, you simply *notice* your muscles and ask yourself, "Are my (shoulders) as relaxed as possible?" I then focus all of my attention on relaxing my shoulders (or any body part) and challenge myself to relax them even more. Then, I do the same with another muscle. These days, I frequently do abbreviated body scans where I just scan my shoulders, jaw, legs, and abdomen, since I tend to carry tension in those areas when I'm anxious or stressed.

COGNITIVE DISTORTIONS

After Dr. Carraway equipped me with those relaxation exercises, she gave me a workbook, which we unpacked together chapter by chapter, week by week. She helped me apply the content to my circumstances, led me through guided practice, and then released me into the week to practice my new skills. In the following session, we'd discuss how my anxiety was that week, and then build on my growing knowledge and skills in the workbook's next chapter. I wish I still had that workbook, but I'm afraid I lent it to a friend who was struggling, and I guess she struggled to return it, and I struggled to notice it was missing until now-ish. Either way, there's a lot of options available today. You can just Google "Cognitive Behavioral Therapy workbook." I've bought a few with intentions to recommend one to you, but it actually turns out that writing a book is already a lot of work. I think it's best to have a therapist walk you through it all, anyway, but access can be messy (more on this in the next chapter), in which case, using a book, e-course, or video series created by a professional can be immensely helpful.

The workbook I used was mostly about cognitive distortions—what they are, how to identify them, and how to escape their control. The first step was learning to notice them, which meant learning to see that rope that dangled down into my mental whirlpools.

I like Dr. Elizabeth Hartney's definition of cognitive distortions:

> [They] are negative or irrational patterns of thinking. These negative thought patterns can play a role in diminishing your motivation, lowering your self-esteem, and contributing to problems like anxiety, depression, and substance use.[4]

There are many different types of cognitive distortions, and before they can be fought, they must be identified, and so below, I'm including a few of my frequent flyers. These were named and explained by Dr. David Burns in his best-selling *Feeling Good Handbook* (1989). He lists far more than these four and goes into greater detail, but I'm afraid of copyright laws (this is my first book), and so if you're interested in learning more, I recommend getting your hands on his book, another CBT workbook, or doing some of your own research online.

One last note before I share my top four cognitive distortions: While some of my thoughts were represented in the examples in my workbook, many were not. It's the ones that relate to my faith that lacked representation twenty years ago. I'm happy to report that in recent years, I discovered a term (thank you, social media) that does: scrupulosity.

> Scrupulosity is a subtype of obsessive compulsive disorder (OCD) involving religious or moral obsessions. Scrupulous individuals are overly concerned that something they thought or did might be a sin or other violation of religious or moral doctrine. They may worry about what their thoughts or behavior mean about who they are as a person.[5]

I'm not saying I have OCD. What I am saying is that I suffer from intrusive scrupulous thoughts that do, in fact, act and feel quite obsessive. Diagnoses like OCD and GAD were made to help people; people were not made to neatly fit diagnoses. They give us frameworks for understanding what happens within our minds (and to an extent, why), but they do not capture the infinitely unique nature of every individual.

That said, to supplement the lack of representation I found in that workbook back in 2007, I am adding examples here from my personal experience that illustrate how cognitive distortions can manifest specifically in the minds of people of faith.

1. All-or-Nothing Thinking AKA: Black-and-White Thinking or Polarized Thinking

Explanation: "See[ing] things in terms of extremes – something is either fantastic or awful, you believe you are either perfect or a total failure."[6]

Scrupulosity: being a spiritual perfectionist, feeling like God's generalized failure, obsessively trying to please God or determine His will

Example from my brain: There is a right song and a wrong song to listen to on the radio. If I choose the right one, God will be pleased with me and I'll experience great joy. If I choose the wrong one, God will be disappointed in me and I'll miss out on a profound spiritual experience and grow further from God.

2. Jumping to Conclusions AKA: Mind Reading

Explanation: "The inaccurate belief that we know what another person is thinking."

Scrupulosity: Praying in a group setting and assuming others are judging you based on your words.

Example from my brain: Sharing something during my mid-week small group and then jumping to the conclusion that my words—intended to heal and encourage—actually destroyed someone, despite my positive intentions.

3. Magnification AKA: Catastrophizing

Explanation: "exaggerating the meaning, importance, or likelihood of things."

Scrupulosity: Catastrophizing how the tiniest misstep can affect eternity

Example from my brain: Whether I sit or stand during musical worship will determine whether my friend encounters Christ or not. Who I decide to eat lunch with today will determine whether or not I have deep fellowship throughout the coming years.

4. "Should" Statements

Explanation: "statements that you make to yourself about what you 'should' do, what you 'ought' to do, or what you 'must' do. They can also be applied to others, imposing a set of expectations that will likely not be met."

Scrupulosity: I should be more emotionally responsive to this worship song.

Example from my brain: I shouldn't be anxious, because decontextualized Bible verses. I must go evangelize to strangers right now or else I'm wasting eternity. I ought to be serving the homeless instead of shopping for curtains right now. I should donate money instead of buying these $10 earrings.

Before I learned about cognitive distortions in therapy, I was clueless that I was drowning in them. My thoughts and emotions were so real and so convincing that I never thought to question them. Dr. Carraway challenged me to identify them as they arose in real time throughout the week. At the end of each day, I'd log them, along with the intensity of the anxiety that accompanied each one. Then, at our next session, we'd review and explore them. Bit by bit, my vision was being restored.

COGNITIVE JOURNALING

To learn to identify my anxious thoughts in real time was to notice that life-saving rope that I kept swirling past. It wasn't enough to simply *see* the distortions; I had to learn how to manipulate and work through them. That's where cognitive journaling came in.

Dr. Carraway trained me through the process, and I don't use the word "train" lightly. Climbing a rope requires strategy and lots of upper body strength, and climbing out of cognitive distortions requires even more strategy and a ton of grit. It's hard to be introspective and level-headed when you're in a whirlpool, and yet most of the time, that's what is needed to use the rope to escape the whirlpool. Recall that "difficulty concentrating" is one of the six characteristics of GAD. Journaling is a particularly helpful strategy when focus is hard to come by: When my mind goes blank or unwanted thoughts intrude, I can simply reread what I wrote and keep moving forward. It allows me to keep putting one hand in front of the other, climbing further and further above the whirlpool, until I'm dripping on solid ground.

I wish I could train you personally like Dr. Carraway trained me, but I'll do what I can by sharing the journaling structure that I was taught (and still use) and by giving you some examples of how I use it. Check out the appendix for a template you can try using, along with two examples you can refer to for guidance.

Before you start journaling, it can be helpful to do some relaxation exercises to lower your physical anxiety. If I have the opportunity, I'll grab a cold, bubbly drink or a piping hot one and start a relaxing playlist. If my body is especially keyed-up, I'll do some squats to burn through some energy. Then I'll take some deep breaths, ask God to help me, and finally put my pen to paper.

I have over a decade's worth of this structured journaling practice scrawled on pages and pages and pages of notebooks and laptops and phones. I still add to them because disorders don't always get entirely cured. Thorns aren't always removed. Thankfully, these strategies I learned 15 years ago are serving me still.

OF THERAPISTS AND THEOLOGIANS

Dr. Carraway taught me how to save myself from my thoughts. She was a God-send. Some Christians take contention here, insisting that only *Christian* counselors qualify as "God-sends" capable of pointing God's children toward healing and Truth. I would like to ask those people, must doctors be Christians for God to heal others through them? Do lawyers need to be Christians for God to exercise justice through them? No! So it is with good therapists and psychiatrists. Regardless of their personal religious or spiritual beliefs, God can use their expertise, training, and gifting to bring healing that many of us so desperately need. As for Dr. Carraway, she did what all good therapists are supposed to do: She respected and worked within my beliefs and values. She made it about me, not her. I told her all sorts of crazy God-related thoughts; she simply helped me see the cognitive distortions at work within them and trained me to pull myself out of them. She never tried to lead me away from my Christianity or advise me in a direction contrary to my faith. The only time her beliefs intersected with mine was in one of our last sessions when she hinted that she, too, believed in God. In her wisdom and humility, Dr. Carraway left my theology to my God and my spiritual leaders, and she stuck to her area of expertise—psychology. She did what I paid her to do: She trained me to pull myself out of anxiety's whirlpool, and in the process, I got my life, mind, and emotions back. Over time, my weekly appointments became biweekly, and then monthly, until she "graduated" me after two years.

Eight years later, in 2017, Patrick and I moved to San Diego, where I found myself sitting across from a new therapist. Let's call her Dr. Buchanan. In our first session, when I mentioned my faith, she exclaimed, "Oh my gosh! I'm a believer too! Wow! This is so great! I think God really planned this! I think I can really help you!" Then she told me about some new Christian song that would really help with my anxiety. I nodded politely as she scribbled its title on a scrap of paper and handed it to me. Then she asked me about my church, and whether we were participating in some national outreach, and if not, I "should look into it because it's going to be a big deal." Towards the end of my session, she told me to light lavender candles, take hot baths, and listen to uplifting worship music. To be blunt, the experience was kind of barfy, and needless to say, I didn't go back. I would much rather have a therapist with ambiguous religious beliefs, like Dr. Carraway, than I would a Christian therapist like Dr. Buchanan who assumes to understand me solely because we share a religion.

A quick word here about finding a therapist: there are Dr. Carraways and there are Dr. Buchanans. And a lot (most?) of them actually aren't "doctors." In fact, "Dr." Buchanan was probably actually Megan Buchanan, LPCC (Licensed Professional Clinical Counselor) or Megan Buchanan, LMFT (Licensed Marriage and Family Therapist). Those are the titles to look for. I've never called a therapist by her first name, like "Megan," or by her "teacher name," Ms. Buchanan, and Dr. Carraway actually had the "Dr." title, so I didn't have to wrestle with what to call her. So let's just stick with the comfortably fictitious name, "Dr. Buchanan." Anyway.

Sometimes you'll click with a therapist, like I did with Dr. Carraway, but it's also possible that you might be disappointed to find yourself sitting across from a Dr. Buchanan instead. And that's okay. The thing is to keep looking until you find one whom you can trust to guide you toward healing. Some people say it's like dating or interviewing potential employees. Like dating, it can be a grueling process, and also like dating, it's helpful to share your journey with your friends. There will likely be insurance to check with, calls to make, and the hardest part, of course, is the fact that you're doing it while suffering through some sort of mental-emotional affliction. And then when you finally meet the therapist, it might be a Dr. Buchanan, which will lead to disappointment and maybe low lows. So, invite your support network into the process so they can support you through it.

All of this Dr. Buchanan business is not to say that Christians cannot be excellent therapists and counselors. I know several who are. A couple years after that failure of a session, I met with a Biblical counselor *on purpose*. She was helping a lot of my friends unpack their pasts and process their trauma. I saw them growing emotionally and spiritually, living more wholly as the beloved children of God they are. I was in a season of persistent anxiety, and I wondered if this counselor, let's call her "Laura," might be able to help me, too. I'd never invited an official "Biblical counselor" into my story, and I wondered whether she might help me see something I hadn't yet. So I reached out.

Laura and I met over Zoom a handful of times. I explained my experience with anxiety, therapy, and medication. Because my anxiety was hitting hard at the time, I wondered out loud whether there might be some hidden, unknown something buried deep inside my heart that was contributing to it. Over the next couple months, Laura helped me explore my family of origin, my identity, and where they intersect with my faith. Although we didn't unearth any shocking revelations, she offered me the kind of insight that sometimes only wise, experienced outsiders can. I'm glad I had her take a look at my soul from her angle.

Depending on the season we're in and who we are, we may need a mentor, a therapist, a psychiatrist, a pastor, a Biblical counselor, a close friend, and always—Jesus. I think the important thing is that we invite people into our struggles. And if we choose our people well, they will point us toward others, too. Like when Patrick pointed to "a professional" so long ago, and when that professional, Dr. Lee, pointed to a Cognitive Behavioral Therapist, Dr. Carraway. And like when my friends, in their vulnerability, shared what they're processing with their counselor, Laura, which inspires me to wonder whether I might have things to process, too. The writer of Proverbs says, "as iron sharpens iron, so one person sharpens another."[7] It is my experience that the more we open our real selves up to loving, wise, humble people, the more fully ourselves we become.

At the end of my first year of Cognitive Behavioral Therapy, Dr. Carraway pointed me back to Dr. Lee. It turned out that my newfound ability to pull myself out of anxious whirlpools wasn't enough. After climbing the rope, I'd sit at the whirlpool's edge on dry ground, soaking wet, catching my breath, when anxiety, like some swim club bully, showed up to shove me back in. Over and over and over again. Every 30 minutes—I'm not exaggerating—a new anxious thought flung me back into the whirlpool, and every time, I'd journal my way out and spend the next 30 minutes catching my breath. And then I'd get shoved in again. And again. It was not a sustainable way to live.

When I told Dr. Carraway about it, she suggested that it might be time to try medication. I was relieved that there was another avenue to explore. Anything for the sake of sanity. Anything to restore reason to its throne. Since prescriptions weren't in her job description, Dr. Carraway messaged Dr. Lee, and his office called me to schedule an appointment.

Chapter 6: Verse

I've kept a journal of sorts since elementary school, long before I learned about Cognitive Journaling. Now decades later, "I've got notebooks full of misshapen words."[1] Most of them are attempts to excavate and explore the roots of complex emotions. They are, largely, the Holy Spirit at work in me. Sometimes, journal entries start as prayer, and other times, they morph into it. Words tend to start as prose and then transform into wild, indecipherable verse. I've attempted to domesticate a few of those poems so that you can interact with them, too. This wildcard of a chapter is the result. These particular poems express my journey through cognitive distortions. I pray they might offer you comfort, clarity, and company on your journey as well.

HYPER AND RESTLESS AND LOST

I used to think
I had to be good enough,
make my life matter enough,
make all the right choices,
discern the elusive will of God
in all things

and approach them with the right heart
and pray often enough,

and fervently enough,
and purely enough

or eternity would crumble
or people wouldn't be saved
or I would be a failure
to my Jesus

and I was so hyper
and restless
and lost

and then one loud night,
the Truth that I somehow lost
flew breathless from the stage
like a paper airplane
—or more like a dove—
through the thick, sweaty darkness
of a Five Iron show:

"All you have to do
is love God
and be who He's made you"

my soul breathed deep
for the first time in weeks

and 20 years later
I need that reminder still—
for I am so prone to
"breaking my back
only to show You
how very lost one can be"[2]

Those words understand me,
and lead me back to the Truth

that His yoke is easy,
and His burden is light

GOD IN THE KITCHEN

He places the butcher knife
Within the reach
Of his four year old daughter

"Chop the onion, kiddo."

She is as terrified
of the gleaming edge
As she is
of letting him down

So she extends her squishy arm,
stretches tiny, trembling fingers
toward the blade
that she just can't wield
and bursts
into tears

I trust my Father
but also,
I am crushed
by the weight of the work
He puts before me

My choice to sit or stand
determines the eternal fate of a friend.
My choice to buy $10 earrings
kills children for want of water
and so my Father
views me
with utter disgust.

But here's the Truth instead—
God is a good,
wise Father,
"mindful that we are but flesh"

Parents like Him
know their kids fully,
And dole out responsibility
accordingly.

He doesn't
toss kitchen knives
toward tiny hands.

He pulls up the step-stool
and invites us
to stir the batter.

He handles knives and ovens
and all the things
beyond us

He simply wants us
`to take joy
and grow
as we work alongside Him

the demanding, critical voice
is a false father—
the disorienting voice
of anxiety.

The Real One is with you
as you fight against it.
He is fighting
for you always.

I AM WEAK.

I used to think I could change the world with machine-like force.
But it turns out I'm weak.
Really weak.
Anxiety-weak.
Overwhelmed-by-tasks-to-the-point-of-inaction weak.
The-house-is-a-mess-and-I'm-not-even-employed weak.
Weak.
Dependent.
Not strong. Helpless.
Incapable of self-care.
A child, or a slightly senile senior,
Often embracing reality
as something it's not,
Expecting myself
to be better
than I am,
Untethered to reality

And isn't that the Truth?
Isn't that me?

But all the while,
I am safe and cared for
Because my Father
lets me sink
into His chest,
a comfort
in utter exhaustion
from the burdens
I compel myself
to carry.

Chapter 7: Medication

"You broke your brain!" Dr. Lee gestured at his head and laughed affably. I awkwardly joined him. It had been a year since he first scribbled me a referral for CBT. Now I was back in his little exam room to discuss medication. He elaborated on my "broken brain" diagnosis: "When our emotions get overused for an extended period of time, our brains can get worn out." He wasn't wrong: as an adolescent and young adult, I spent gallons of tears on friends and family, and some on myself, too. Plus, my brain did feel kind of broken.

He moved on to next-steps and explained, "Antidepressants aren't just for depression; they are also effective at treating anxiety. There are a lot of different varieties, and everyone responds to them differently. The first one we try might be 'the one,' or it might not be. So don't worry if it's not 'the one,' okay? We can try different ones until we find what works for you." I nodded. "I'm going to start you on a low dose of Prozac. It's a very common antidepressant. A lot of people use it for anxiety. How does that sound?"

"It sounds good." I kept nodding.

"Now, you won't notice a difference right away. It takes time for it to build up in your body. You might start feeling some improvement in about two weeks. Also, we don't start with the full dosage. We start small and monitor how you're doing, and then we can add to it. So I want you to come back in two weeks so we can see how you're doing and if we need to adjust the dosage, okay?"

"Okay, yah, that makes sense."

"Do you have any questions for me?"

"No. Sounds good! Thank you!"

"Okay, see you in two weeks! Take care!"

I left with a prescription and hope.

Every two weeks, I returned to check in with Dr. Lee until I was at a fairly high dose of Prozac. It had been a couple months, and I was kind of disappointed that I wasn't feeling much better. No bad side-effects, but my frequent anxiety episodes hadn't really decreased, either. So Dr. Lee tapered me off of it, and we went through the same process with a similar antidepressant, Zoloft.

A couple weeks in, I was feeling a difference, and a couple months in, I was relieved that my anxiety episodes had become far less frequent. Twenty anxiety attacks a day became two. When I used my strategies to pull myself out of anxiety whirlpools, I got to actually stay out long enough to dry off. Eventually, I experienced entire days without anxiety and realized that my disorder was no longer disordering my life. I began to enjoy teaching and discovered great meaning in my work. I built positive relationships with my students and laughed with them a lot. The work was still challenging, and anxiety still made its appearances, but when it did, I was able to belly breathe and journal it away. It was manageable.

It was around this time that Dr. Carraway graduated me from therapy. At our last session, she said I made her feel successful, which made me feel good enough to remember it today, 15 years later. I don't really remember her other words, except for this prophecy at the end of our session: "Now, Tiffany, don't be surprised if this all comes back when you have a significant life change, like moving, or a change in your career, or starting a family." I nodded solemnly and kept those words. We hugged, I thanked her, and I left feeling grateful for my growth.

I had a few good months after that, but then the anxiety attacks reappeared out of the blue, as if I had stopped taking my medication. I hadn't, though. I was scared to tell Dr. Lee. It felt like admitting that I was beyond fixing, that even medication wouldn't work for me. I feared, *What if he says that there are no more medicines to try? What if I am just a straight-up wreck who is going to feel this way forever? What if an institution awaits?*

With no other options, I sucked it up, called his office, and braced myself for my hopeless prognosis. At the appointment, when he asked me how I was doing, I confessed, "I'm doing okay, but it feels like my medication stopped working. The anxiety came back."

"Ahhh." He nodded his head. "Sometimes, people's bodies adjust to the medication and build a tolerance to it. I think that's what happened to you. I want to try an antidepressant that works a little differently than the first two. It's called an SNRI. The kinds you had before were SSRI's."

"Ok," I responded. I recalled the terms from a neurobiology course I took in college.

"I'm going to prescribe you a low dose of Effexor and wean you off of the Zoloft. Schedule an appointment for two weeks and we'll see how you're doing then."

"Ok, thank you!"

"Bye now, take care!"

I was relieved. Hope still remained.

Every two weeks, Dr. Lee increased my dose of Effexor, and week by week, my anxiety became more manageable. Unfortunately, when we hit 225 mg, the maximum outpatient dosage, I still wasn't experiencing the same relief I initially had with Zoloft.

I feared my final follow-up appointment. I wished I could give Dr. Lee the good news we'd hoped for. I imagined dramatic next-steps: *Would I be sent to an institution where I could receive a higher dose? Would that be my life now? Sequestered from society? Would my parents have to visit me there? Was I that broken?*

When doomsday arrived, I was ruminating in exam room number two when the door swung open and Dr. Lee appeared.

"Hi! How's it going? How have you been feeling?"

"Hi! I'm better than I was two weeks ago, but I'm still having some anxiety."

"Hm, well you're at the maximum dosage for the Effexor, so what we can do is—" I braced myself for *"refer you to an inpatient program."*

"—try adding a second medication. It's called Wellbutrin. It's like a booster for other antidepressants. It helps a lot of people."

"Oh, phew!" I confessed, "I was afraid I was going to be out of options and have to become an inpatient somewhere!"

He chuckled lightly. "Oohh, no, no, no! There are many, many options!" he reassured me. "Don't worry about that!"

On my way home, I filled my new prescription. Like the other pills, we increased my Wellbutrin dosage bit by bit until, to my relief, I was back to my normal, less-anxious self. I felt like me again. I stuck with that Effexor-Wellbutrin pair for the next five years, until Dr. Carraway's prophecy became my reality: that "significant life change" hit when we moved to San Diego, and as she warned, GAD came crashing back into my life, like Kool-Aid Man through a brick wall. But that's a story for another chapter.

WHOLE: MIND, BODY, AND SPIRIT

I don't take the phrase, "the miracle of modern medicine" lightly. The intricacies of our brains, our physiologies, our universe, are embossed with the fingerprint of a Maker in whose image we are made. God had it in mind that society by society, century by century, His daughters and sons would experiment and research and unveil, bit by bit, some of the knowledge by which He built everything. As we are made in the Creator's image, we too create, explore, and wonder.

Our steadily growing knowledge has led us to here and now: satellites and smartphones and liver transplants and printed kidneys and everything else the future holds. Antidepressants are among those creations. The pills stand on millenia of scientific progress, birthed through the pains and passions of scientists and their supporters. I like to think that some of those scientists had people like me in mind as they tinkered in their labs—people whose lives would be profoundly improved by their equations and formulas and trials.

While we all benefit from the offerings of scientific progress, we don't all benefit equally from all of it. Organ transplants are for humanity, but they aren't for everyone. Same with antidepressants. They are for me, but they aren't for everyone. Just because medication is available does not mean it is appropriate.

Oftentimes, anxiety has roots that are not grounded in a physiological disorder. It can surface in response to unprocessed trauma, stunted emotional growth, spiritual immaturity, and/or deeply embedded lies we've soaked in for years. It is often a messy mix of all of that, and the thing is, medication does not cure or solve any of those underlying issues. I liken medicating trauma to putting Anbesol on a cavity. It can calm the pain temporarily, and it can tide you over until you can make it to the dentist, but if you rely on it to avoid the discomfort of the drill, then that deeply rooted infection will eventually worsen and take over.

I suppose that's one reason why Dr. Lee sent me to therapy before he sent me to the pharmacy: while psychiatric medication can ease symptoms on its own to an extent, true healing from practically all mental disorders also requires the hard work of therapy. For most of us, however, it's far more comfortable to swallow a pill than it is to let a therapist aim light at the cobwebbed corners of our souls. But if that deep work isn't done, medication can become an enabler that perpetuates avoidance and harms our human wholeness.

My friend, Julio, has a story that illustrates this. He is a retired Puerto Rican American who spent 35 years in law enforcement as a Marine, Border Patrol Agent, and Air Marshal. Such a career basically *promises* exposure to trauma. After decades of service, he slowed down and traded in combat for paperwork. Ironically, that's when he started having panic attacks. On several occasions, he ended up in the emergency room where he was prescribed pills for his anxiety, but not informed about Panic Disorder or the PTSD from which he was suffering. No one directed him to therapy. The medication gave him negative side effects which only made things worse for him and his family. He and his wife separated. He became estranged from his adult daughter. It was a tragic spiral, one that is far too commonplace for men and women in his line of work.

His trajectory changed one night when a woman on an infomercial, of all things, described his symptoms. She was selling mindfulness DVDs, and he ordered the collection. Julio practiced what he learned and got noticeable relief from his symptoms. He saw a new doctor who took him off the medication his previous doctor put him on. Julio then sought out a Christian counselor with whom he ended up working for years. As a result, Julio's life and relationships slowly and steadily improved. Today, 10 years later, he and his wife, daughter, and grandchildren are living healthy, peaceful lives together.

Many people know stories like Julio's. His is a cautionary tale of addressing the body without addressing the mind and spirit. This is not to say that antidepressants can't aid in the process of therapy, but they certainly can't substitute for it. Keyed-up nervous systems sometimes benefit from medication so that people can focus on the work of therapy instead of being stuck in a constant state of fight, flight, or freeze. Medication can help set a safer, more effective stage for feeling difficult feelings and working through traumatic events. It can supplement motivation and energy levels so that there's enough to keep showing up for sessions. It's a complicated thing to navigate, which is why it is essential to work with professionals.

On the opposite end of Julio's experience is April's. We met on the Pufferfish soccer team in sixth grade. April is a freckled brunette with a contagious smile, a fun-loving spirit, a kind heart, and an excellent sense of humor. We were instant friends. At 42, we still are. At the surface, April does not seem like a depressed person, but in her own words, she's "battled a difficult thought life and lowness [her] whole life."

Not unlike me, her mental health suffered most in her 20's and 30's. She was in therapy on-and-off. She explains,

> I was nervous, unable to think clearly. Negative. I felt like everyone was against me. I felt voiceless. I felt extremely low energy, hard to get moving at any point during the day. I felt very down—occasionally so down that I just wanted to make it all stop... but I couldn't even fathom going *there*, so I just suffered through the deep pain and hoped each next day would be better.
>
> After having a desperate low episode in my mid 20's, I did try Zoloft. The medication seemed to really help stabilize me (no more low lows), but it also made me feel flat. I didn't laugh or cry. I just was *there*, sorta. So after about nine months, I stopped taking it.
>
> Despite the signs and symptoms, it was really hard to admit to myself that I felt depressed. It felt shameful to be a depressed person. What did I have to be depressed about? To me, depression was basically synonymous with being ungrateful. I just wasn't thankful enough. I wasn't strong

enough, and I just wasn't able to roll up my sleeves and get my crap together. I was being weak.

Despite making progress in therapy, April continued to struggle. Professionals encouraged her to try medication again, as did I, but thanks to some childhood trauma and a steady stream of parental gaslighting early in life, she refused it.

April white-knuckled her way through her depression until her mid-30's, when her low lows struck again. She was pregnant with her second child when, at an OBGYN appointment, she confided in her nurse practitioner about her depression. She agreed with her NP's recommendation to try an antidepressant. However, when she got home and noticed the little sticker on the bottle that said, "Talk to your doctor if you are pregnant or nursing," she let the pills expire in her medicine cabinet.

Her sadness didn't stop, but she persisted. She continued therapy, where she worked through a lot of the trauma that was responsible for her refusal to take psychiatric medication in the first place. When she stopped nursing her third and last child, she decided to give antidepressants another chance. Her doctor prescribed Prozac. When I asked her about her mental health recently, she said this:

> Prozac has changed my life. I feel secure. Self-assured. I feel like I can do hard things without trying super hard. I feel like I can be thankful automatically rather than forcing myself to try really hard. I can think straight. I can (mostly) keep my house clean and organized without a weekly housekeeper. I can make decisions—even big ones.
>
> I love myself. I even love others! I don't yell uncontrollably. I have way more self control. I no longer drink daily to numb my emotions and feel better. I do things I enjoy and don't feel bad about it.

Many Christians like April with access to professional help endure crippling depression and anxiety while refusing to try medication for a plethora of reasons. We'll get into them in chapter 11, but here, it's worth mentioning that stigma is a major factor, as is misinformation, deeply rooted bias, negative past experiences, and fear of side-effects, which are especially relevant for young mothers like April. When I asked her what advice she'd give mothers in her shoes, April said she'd encourage them to do what the pill bottles say and actually *talk* to their doctors about risks and benefits, along with doing their own research before deciding that antidepressants are off the table for them.

Mind, body, and spirit cannot be separated. In Julio's case, the hospitals he went to for panic attacks gave him pills without guidance toward therapeutic resources. His malady was addressed physically, but not mentally or spiritually. Once he started practicing mindfulness through those mail-order DVDs and meeting regularly with a Christian counselor, he truly healed. In April's case, the therapists she saw for years addressed her mind, and Christian mentors and friends addressed her spirit, but her body remained in need until she found the antidepressant that worked for her.

Mind, body, and spirit all play essential roles in our ability to function; each facet is deeply nuanced, contributing to the complex, whole people we are. Each aspect of ourselves spills into the others. For that reason, when things go awry, we need good diagnosticians, especially doctors and mental health professionals, along with the support and wise counsel of friends, pastors, and mentors.

If you're concerned that your doctor might make a decision like Julio's did and prematurely send you away with a prescription, then write questions and concerns down and bring them to your appointment. You can also bring a loved one to advocate for you, especially if your mental-emotional health is compromised. Take April's advice to work through biases, and try your best to keep an open mind.

ON BEING RELIANT

I'll admit that it doesn't feel great to be reliant on an outside source for my ability to function. The what-ifs of the future are not lost on me: *What if society melts down to a Mad Max consistency? I won't be able to get my pills. What if we land in the zombie apocalypse? No pills there, either. What if all progress gets crushed by a modern equivalent of the burning of the Alexandrian library, and civilization rewinds to the Dark Ages? Tylenol would become rare gems, and antidepressants would go extinct! How would I cope without my pills? Could I even take care of myself? Would anyone be willing to take care of me?* Reliance on anything or anyone requires an admission that I am not as independent as I'd like to be. It's an unsettling reality.

Needing medication does not, however, make me any different from the rest of humanity. Most people don't like to think about this, but despite our superfoods, our workout routines, our positivity—despite all our admirable efforts—Covid reminded us that we are all still vulnerable to microscopic viruses, loneliness, supply chain disruptions, weak economies, volatile governments, systemic corruption, widespread violence, and all the trauma and darkness festering deep within each of us. The pandemic confronted us with the Truth that the hobbies, habits, and routines we rely on for pleasure and distraction can be taken away. Our physical and mental health can also be taken away. That disturbing Truth triggers anxiety for many of us, regardless of whether or not we have a disorder.

Pandemics and wars and rumors of wars test our foundations, and it turns out that most foundations are built on sand. Practically everything in this world is capable of letting us down, including the people who promise not to. So what is left to build on? Many choose to build on themselves and their happiness. But that too can crumble, and that's a lot of pressure to put on yourself.

I think the best thing we can do is make peace with the fact that we don't get to determine our own fates. It's up to Someone far better. We can work toward goals, and even achieve a lot of them, but the only foundation for deep inner-peace is Jesus Christ, the divine person who said, "whoever wants to save their life will lose it, but whoever loses their life for me will find it."[1] Perhaps "losing our lives" means holding our desires and plans with open hands toward Jesus in a gesture of "not my will, but Yours be done."[2]

MOSH PITS AND COFFEE SHOPS

My brain is normally a coffee shop where God and I meet to talk. It's the kind of place that plays lofi and acoustic music. Its aesthetics are warm and cozy, like a cabin nestled in the redwoods. It smells like steaming lattes and spiced blueberry muffins, and it buzzes with passionate, hushed conversations. It's a place where I can interact with Jesus and concentrate and question and listen and feel my feelings. It's a place for shedding light in the dark corners of my soul and exploring what's there. It's a place where He gives me words for things unspoken.

But during anxiety attacks, that coffee shop transforms into a chaotic punk rock venue. Tables and chairs are kicked over to make room for the mosh pit, and blaring amps destroy all conversation and make the walls rumble.

I like a good punk show as much as the next Five Iron Frenzy fan, but it's basically the worst possible place to talk. Everyone goes mute. To be heard, you need to cup your friend's ear and use all your lungs to yell something like, "I'M GONNA GO PEE!" Attempting to say anything more risks taking an elbow to the throat because mosh pits are demanding.

Anxiety is demanding, too. The sheer panic of it prevents me from having focused, nuanced conversations with anyone, be it Jesus, a best friend, or a new one. And I can't concentrate on what I read either, be it a Bible or a textbook. When anxious, most of my prayer life amounts to some version of "GOD, SAVE ME!"

At the start of my journey through GAD, I was stuck in that mosh pit for a long time, and I didn't understand why. I was distraught over the alarming change in my ability to concentrate. I thought the change in my prayer and reading life were all my fault. I thought it was all because of some unknown sin I had to find. Confusion and guilt fueled desperate, futile efforts to feel the way I did when Jesus and I met in the coffee shop.

Although I felt far from Him, God never left the building. He was right there with me in the mosh pit. It was there that I learned to cup my hands around His ear and yell my desperate pleas. As a result, we bonded in a way that only happens in mosh pits. And plus, the thing about God is that He doesn't need the physics of sound to understand me, anyway. He understands my thoughts from afar,[3] and He never leaves me nor forsakes me.[4]

Over time and therapy and medication, the punk rock venue transformed back into the coffee shop, and my medication helps maintain it. It helps my brain and body function like they're meant to, which helps me commune with God like I'm meant to. It is not a substitute for difficult soul-work, but rather, it equips me to do better soul-work. The purpose of antidepressants is not to numb the emotions of the masses, but rather to restore order to minds muddled by chaos. It's not pursue Christ *or* take medication. Rather, for people like myself, it is both. Sometimes, seeing a psychiatrist is what it looks like to "love the Lord your God with all your mind."[5]

"PRAY WITH EACH PILL"

Effective medication is a common grace from God, a vehicle through which He delivers healing in this world of common pain. Sometimes these days, when I take my two-toned capsules at night, I celebrate. Before I pop them in my mouth, I hold them up to my ear and give them a little shake. I listen to the tiny beads rattle around inside and think about how my Cymbalta would make a great percussion instrument for Ratatouille. I thank God for the tiny miracles that somehow empower my mind and body to function like they were created to.

Recently on Instagram, I came across a post about prayers and pills by therapist and author, K.J. Ramsey, and I can't think of any better way to close this chapter than with her words:

> Thirteen years ago, when I filled my first prescription for a disease that didn't yet have a name, my grandma called with some advice.
>
> 'Pray with each pill,' she said.
>
> I think I started swallowing a better story about where God is in my struggles that day.
>
> God doesn't just heal in miraculous moments, when the seemingly right alchemy of passion and prayer instantly turns our pain to praise.
>
> God pervades even our pills. Divine love permeates the covalent bonds forming this medicine and the bonds of compassion connecting doctor to patient, therapist to client, and friend to friend.
>
> I watch for the slow miracles. I exalt the God of small things. I pay attention to the warm light from my window like a benediction and I wrap the kindness of friends around me like a blanket against the cold of losing hope.
>
> And now, holding yet another bottle of pills for a new, serious endocrine disorder, I am remembering that these hands that have lifted more than a lifetime's worth of pills and uncertainty can still raise a prayer of slow and steady hope.
>
> Because though it's just me
>
> swallowing these pills,
>
> it's not just me enduring this story.

So, here is my benediction

for all who suffer long:

Let each pill be a prayer.

(Antidepressants included.)

May you swallow solidarity and hope whole.

May your eyes glimpse, even this week, Christ is *with* you—in the generosity of a friend, the surprising kindness of a doctor, or the smile of a stranger.

May your gaze find, even this weekend, Christ is *in* you—in the faith and compassion you extend toward your own body, in the vulnerability you allow someone to see like a cross lifted up in the middle of this world.

Miracles remain in your midst.

(And, your endurance, it is one of the mightiest.)

Chapter 8: Version 2.0

Her words felt like a prophecy: "Now, Tiffany, don't be surprised if all this anxiety comes back when you have a significant life change…"

The fulfillment of Dr. Carraway's prophecy hit seven years later, in 2017 when Patrick started a new career that moved us 455 miles south of the San Francisco Bay Area, where we both grew up, to San Diego, where we knew nobody.

I quit my job at the high school I had been teaching at for 11 years. Because it was easy to land that job, and because the phrase "teacher shortage" was a thing, I figured I'd find a new school to settle into with ease. I started applying to school districts while finishing my last year of teaching up north. Despite applying to every district within an hour's drive of our new place in San Diego, I only got one interview. I bought a plane ticket and flew down for it.

It turned out to be a group interview with a PE teacher and a Kindergarten teacher. This is not common practice for an English teacher in the education world. It was weird. It went well, though, until the end when our interviewer casually wrapped it up with this:

"Thank you all for your time. We don't have any positions available at this time, but we will keep you updated."

What?!?! Why hold job interviews if there's no jobs?! I bought a flight for this?! I was flabbergasted, and I almost said it. But then I remembered my employment goal, so I kept my mouth shut, gave the interviewer a smile, a handshake, and flew back up north.

Five months later, after the next school year had already begun without me, an HR representative called with not one job offer, but three. I chose a position teaching English and art (which I'm not even credentialed for) at a small satellite campus of a continuation high school. It's one of those schools where students go when they get too many "F's" in traditional high school. Thankfully, classes were small and the community felt a little like family. I got to create my own curriculum, and I worked hard to help build my students' confidence and skills. Despite the constant stream of ants on our portable classroom's walls, I did my best to transform our space into a second (or first) home for my kiddos. My role felt like 50% life coaching and 50% teaching, a balance that fit my motivation for becoming a teacher: to help the kids who don't have the help they need.

Unfortunately, my anxiety disorder was also blowing up in my face. I felt like I did before I started medication, which was particularly distressing because *I was still on my medication.* My relentless swim club bully stomped back into my life, shoving me into the anxiety whirlpool over and over and over again, leaving me clinging to the edge of the pool, gasping for air.

Something about the water in the whirlpool felt different, though. I had new symptoms. Gone were the tingles in my hands and the circling thoughts in my mind. Instead, my legs and chest burned bright red, hot to the touch. Well-intentioned people pointed out that I was "sunburned" from time to time. My heart pounded and palpitated so wildly and so often that I ended up wearing a holster with wires taped all over my chest for 24 hours of monitoring. I was also tested for a thyroid disorder. Both came back negative. Generalized Anxiety Disorder alone was to blame.

ANXIOUS IN PARADISE

I took a lot of deep breaths to make it through my workdays, and on Fridays, to unwind, I'd detour to a nearby beachfront farmers market for dinner and peace of mind. It was a glorious setup. Like Toucan Sam, I followed my nose through a United Nations of food booths: curries, empanadas, crepes, Korean BBQ, Mexican corn, and a bunch of desserts that I wished weren't gluten-free.

On one particular Friday, I chose three little empanadas and settled onto my beach blanket. I took in the endless ocean, did some belly breathing, savored the flavors, and connected with the rhythmic crashing of the waves. A seagull challenged me to a stare-down over my guava empanada and won the last bite.

I got up to wander the shore and watch the sun sink into the horizon. I started to pray because it felt right. What better place to connect with the Creator, right?

Wrong.

Right then, my throat cramped, which meant the anxiety faucet was cranking on. My annoyance bordered on defeat. *Why does it have to happen *now*?*

As expected, the other symptoms came crashing in. My chest and legs flushed red. My heart pounded and palpitated. My muscles tensed. My mental health crumbled. I couldn't help but think, *If I can't have peace now, I never will!*

I felt like a broken human—sunset at the beach is supposed to make me heal, not disintegrate.

I have since learned that this version of anxiety is called "free-floating anxiety." It is marked by

> a pervasive sense of unease, tension, or nervousness that isn't specifically tied to any particular situation, event, or

trigger. Individuals experiencing free-floating anxiety may feel on edge, worried, or anxious without knowing exactly why.[1]

The worst part is that this new free-floating anxiety stripped me of my best weapon against anxiety attacks: cognitive journaling. If you check out the template and examples in the appendix (pages 206-211), you'll see that these are the first steps:

1. Identify and rate the intensity of the emotion you're feeling.
2. Identify the situation you were in when you started feeling that way.
3. Write down the automatic thoughts you were having.

And that's where the problem hit. My new form of anxiety didn't come with automatic thoughts. In the past, my anxious thoughts played on repeat with the volume cranked up. There was never a question about what they were, so when I journaled, I was able to find evidence supporting and refuting them, which usually freed me from them.

Since moving to San Diego, though, my automatic thoughts all but disappeared. They struck like lightning—here one second and gone the next—sparking lasting, uncontrollable wildfires in my body. I was only able to perceive my thoughts on some vague, subconscious level of guesswork.

Despite my anxiety's comeback and its regular drop-ins at the continuation school, I felt good about the work I was doing there. I was looking forward to improving upon it the following year. But in May, one of my colleagues, Mr. Lawson, appeared in my doorway at the end of my last class. He is a tall, gray-haired social studies teacher my age with a healthy sense of humor and a kind demeanor. He said, "Heeey, Ms. Ciccone, can I talk with you outside for a minute?"

In a hushed voice, he asked, "Hey, what kind of contract do you have?"

"Uh, I don't know... probationary?"

"You should check. I think it's temporary."

"Really? I don't think so... I've never even heard of a temporary teaching contract."

"You should check, because I'm pretty sure it is." He gave me a compassionate look that said, *I'm so sorry.*

Sure enough, he was right. My contract expired in a matter of weeks, and then I was flung into unemployment.

I grieved the classroom-home I had been building for my students and myself. I applied for positions for the next school year, but heard nothing. I didn't understand my purpose. My medication wasn't working anymore. My anxiety was at an all-time high, and I felt lost.

Each day demanded the entirety of my emotional and mental energy. Moment by moment, the fibers of my spiritual muscles tore, and Jesus was there, rebinding them, teaching me how to live with the Truth that I am not in control—not of my mental health, and not of my career. He was training me to "take my long-term plans somewhat lightly and work from moment to moment 'as to the Lord,'" because that's all I could do.[2] He was teaching me to endure and trust His process. In that season, these words by Scott Erickson found me on Instagram and gave me hope:

> Sometimes it's summer flourishing. Sometimes it's outwardly dead like winter. But in every winter there are hidden developments working their way to an eventual spring. Give yourself time. Let that which is hidden do its work.[3]

As a gardener who knows what it is to dig deep through hard ground in October, drop in dead-looking bulbs, and see no evidence of growth until March, Scott's words hit hard. I was the bulb in October, six inches underground, and I was also the gardener with nothing to see for the work she had put in. I needed the reminder that just because I couldn't see life emerging, that didn't mean it wasn't. As the bulb, I couldn't see my purpose. I was just an ugly, dry, wrinkled thing enduring. I didn't know what I was becoming, or how and when I would contribute beauty and life to the world. I couldn't sense the endurance God was growing in my soul, or the fruit that would one day ripen and offer hope to others.

GETTING PRAYER

Over the course of our first year in San Diego, Patrick and I settled into a small church in our community called Restored South Bay. At the time, it was a two-year-old, non-denominational church of about 100 or so people who met at an elementary school on Sundays and at people's homes for small groups during the week. The demographic was ethnically diverse and young-ish, which (when you're a 42-year old author) means a lot of people were in their late 20's and 30's.

Because I was stuck in such a rough survival season, I decided to do something brave and desperate one Sunday: I decided to ask for prayer for my anxiety. At Restored, that looks like approaching a leader who's standing in the front during the closing worship songs. My eyes landed on Rae, a friendly social worker who I met a couple weeks prior. Her profession gave me hope that she probably understood mental illness better than most. Still, I wasn't sure that opening up to a church person about my anxiety disorder was a good idea. Past experiences warned me against it, but I'd noticed this new church culture was different. People practiced vulnerability and admitted their weaknesses, especially the pastors.

I hoped Rae might be safe. I hoped she wouldn't ask God to help me trust Him. I hoped she wouldn't force a sermon or advice through her prayer. I hoped to be understood and supported. I hoped she might fulfill Jesus' command to "bear one another's burdens," because mine was getting too heavy to carry alone.[4]

I got up from my folding chair and made my way to the front where Rae stood. She greeted me warmly, placed her hand on my shoulder, and leaned in to listen. My eyes watered as I let the truth spill from my lips: "I have an anxiety disorder, and it's been really hard lately."

The expression on Rae's face invited me to say more. "I'm really anxious right now, and I can't get it to stop, and I'm just really tired from it. It's been bad since we moved down here."

Rae's response is best explained by the words of Maya Angelou: "People will forget what you said, people will forget what you did, but people will never forget how you made them feel." I forget most of what Rae said before she prayed, but a few words of her prayer haven't left me. It went something like this:

"Lord, thank you for Tiffany... and Lord, thank you for your hand in her life. This anxiety, it's not a surprise to you. You knew she'd struggle with this. You know how hard it is. And You are with her in the midst of it."

I was surprised by the comfort those words brought me. They reminded me that I am entirely known by God, and that He is entirely present with me in anxiety and in tranquility. He knows that together, we can handle it. And by "together" I mean "mostly so far it's all been You."[5] I'm still under His sovereign care, which means "it is well with my soul."[6] Rae affirmed that it's okay for me to struggle. Through her, God reminded me that He looks at me with compassion and empathy and scoops me up in His love. I'm not in it alone. He is as present with me now as he has been through my entire story. Through Rae, the Spirit reminded me that my story is One, that God is One, and that He is Love. I didn't feel so alone anymore. For the first time, I felt unashamed, understood, and embraced as a believer with an anxiety disorder.

It was the start of a new season. The Spirit used Rae's prayer, Restored's practice of vulnerability, and a decade of anxiety to flip a switch in me: I no longer cared. I'd been through all the anxiety before, and I was over it. I was over the stigma. I was convinced of the reality of my struggle. I no longer cared if people misjudged. The spirit of table-flipping overcame me, I suppose.[7] The previous year, I had started a blog and written a few posts about anxiety, so I was already equipped with some words. A voice was ignited within me. I was fed up and ready to speak out. So I did.

I kept writing and sharing on social media, which took some guts because that's where the people from my past listen to my present. I had so much to say, so much built up over those 10 years. I spoke openly. I didn't care who knew I took antidepressants. I didn't care who knew about my disorder. And as I let the Truth leak out, other people started speaking to me about their mental health struggles, too.

A new friend from Restored, Julian, was the first believer I heard describe anxiety like mine. Ten years. That's how long it took me to meet another person at that messy intersection of faith and mental illness. It was so lonely for so long. Julian's commiseration and camaraderie strengthened my resolve to speak about my experience. His story confirmed what I suspected all along: I was never alone.

Looking back, I owe the developmental stages of this book to that "lifeless" period of free-floating anxiety and professional instability. When I felt lost and purposeless, I got the image of Jesus standing down a path, waving me toward him, saying, "C'mmon. Let's keep going. Let's keep writing." It was enough to motivate me to drive to coffee shops and work from moment to moment on my laptop, clueless as to what it might or might not amount to. I'm still not sure what it will amount to. But the point is faithfulness, which is something I learned as a bulb.

ACCESS AND SELF-MEDICATION

When I was seeking spiritual support for my anxiety, I was also seeking medical support. It wasn't very easy to do because my inconsistent employment caused inconsistent insurance coverage. When I finally met with a primary doctor, I told her about my heart palpitations and anxiety. She referred me to a cardiologist and ordered some bloodwork.

Before she left the exam room, I added, "Oh, also, I take antidepressants for my anxiety and I need some refills."

She glanced down at the papers I filled out in the waiting room and then looked up abruptly.

Then she decisively said, "No. No, I'm not comfortable managing these."

"What?" I asked in disbelief. *There must be some confusion*, I thought. But then she repeated what she said. I was agape. I tried explaining things to correct her confusion: "My old primary doctor prescribed my Effexor and Wellbutrin... It was no problem." But she just looked at me. "So what am I supposed to do?"

"I'm going to refer you to psychiatry." She highlighted the number I needed to call on my check-out form.

"Ok... But I only have a couple days of medication left. Can you just prescribe me some refills just to get me by?"

"Ok, fine. I'm writing you a one month refill of each; then you need to work with the psychiatrist, ok?"

"Yeah, ok," I said, annoyed. I was already resolved to find a new primary doctor.

The next day, I called the psychiatrist's office to schedule an appointment. Over the phone, I waited as the receptionist clicked through her calendar, until she offered me her first opening—in May! It was only *November*.

"Wait, your next appointment isn't until *May*? That's like six months away!"

"Yeah, sorry, we're really booked. That's the earliest appointment I have for new patient intake."

"Well, I guess I'll take it...I don't know what I'll do in the meantime."

She gave me a number I could call in case of a psychiatric emergency. Then we hung up. There were no other options. I had an HMO, and staying in-network meant using this organization.

I picked up the phone and immediately called that primary doctor in a panic: "I called the Psychiatric Center and I scheduled the earliest appointment available, but it's six months out! Can you please prescribe me the refills I need until I have my appointment?"

...she sighed...and then nothing...

I started to plead: "I don't know what else to do—I really need them! My old primary doctor up north prescribed them to me for years with no problems, I promise! You can look up my records! I've been on these pills for over five years! I'm really afraid of what will happen to me if I just go off of them all of a sudden! Effexor has really bad withdrawal symptoms! Like, I missed a couple doses once because of insurance issues and I was dizzy and crying for no reason!" My voice was getting shaky. I was incredulous that I was having to explain these things to a *doctor*.

Finally, she conceded with another sigh and an "Okay."

I was relieved. Although my medication was barely effective anymore, it was certainly better than the "brain zaps" and suicidal thoughts some people experience when they quit Effexor cold turkey.

THERAPY 2.0

In that six-month extended anxiety disaster, I did find one other thing I could do while I waited to see a psychiatrist: find a therapist in my new area. I hoped that perhaps Dr. Carraway forgot to teach me something really important. I didn't really believe that, but I hoped it, so I reached out and left messages with 12 local therapists in my insurance network. Of them, only two returned my calls, and of the two, only one was accepting new clients.

I was dumbfounded. Was this the norm? How can this be the system that serves people who are desperate for help?

I met with the only available therapist. At the end of our first session, she told me that I already knew all of the CBT stuff she teaches clients like me. So much for help. I had two or three sessions with her, from which I gained a couple nuggets:

> Nugget 1: She taught me the phrase, "Don't should on yourself," which is helpful for remembering and fun to say in groups.

> Nugget 2: She pointed out that because my anxiety is mostly somatic, or physical, it should be attacked on the somatic front. This made sense.

I followed her advice and tried all the things to fix my anxious body, short of adjusting my meds, which was the thing I really needed to do but couldn't thanks to that long waitlist. I tried a few yoga sessions. I started jogging again. I discovered that squats and high-knees can be particularly helpful for releasing pent-up anxious energy. I researched diet and anxiety and tweaked my eating. I drank cold bubbly drinks and hot steamy teas to soothe my insides. I practiced deep breathing and progressive muscle relaxation. I used lavender and peppermint oils. I got more sleep. While all of these things bring healing, in that season, they weren't enough for me. I still needed what I couldn't get.

I was learning that most paths to professional help curve up steep, rocky mountains. Many travelers collapse by the side of the road. I am a privileged white woman with a master's degree and two loving parents who were able to help Patrick and I buy our first house. When I was diagnosed with GAD a decade ago, I got to take the chairlift up the mountain to quality care, thanks to my privileges: a PPO, a low co-pay for antidepressants, a primary doctor I'd had for 15 years, and money to pay for my $120 therapy sessions.

Ten years later in San Diego, I was missing two of those things: a PPO and a good primary doctor. I still had plenty of advantages, but just those two missing links were enough to prevent me from obtaining timely help. How much more difficult it must be for people in poverty to access mental health care!

After my first teaching job in San Diego, I taught at four more high schools over the following seven years. Every new school came with new courses (seventeen in all!), new cultures and demographics, new campus procedures, new departmental expectations, new platforms, and new steep learning curves to claw my way up. Most of the time, positions were offered *after* the school year began, which meant practically no onboarding or training. I have been plunged into classrooms before receiving a laptop, passwords, supplies, or any paid time to prep.

The teaching scene in San Diego is impacted and some districts are disasters. Almost all of the available contracts are temporary, which means that every June, we new teachers get tossed back into unemployment. We endure (to the extent that we can) without health benefits over the summers, without job security, and without any opportunity to build meaningful relationships with colleagues or get really good at teaching any particular course. It's great for anxiety.

Growing up, I had a betta fish. A few, actually. (But not all at once. I'm not a sadist.) Whenever I cleaned their fish bowl and poured some freshly treated water in, they'd freak out. Freeze up. Their fins, normally limp and relaxed, would stand taut and straight. Their scales would become more pale. But after a minute, they would begin to relax, explore, and continue being their regular fishy selves.

Every time I started teaching at a new school, I felt like one of those betas. More days than not, for the first few months of a new teaching assignment, I'd have anxiety attacks. As I spent more time in my new ~~fishbowl~~ classroom, I'd relax a bit. My fins un-tensed. The anxiety attacks became less frequent, and I returned to my normal teachery self. Until my contract ended and the cycle resumed at some other school.

Anyway. All of this is to say that I have taught in inner-cities, suburbia, and affluence: at a school surrounded by a moat of trash and dirty diapers, and a school surrounded by palm trees, golden plaques, and lawn bowling. At schools that hosted rats and ants in classrooms, and a school that hosted a stress-relief petting zoo during state testing week.

Generally speaking, poverty breeds trauma. Kids in under-resourced urban communities endure far more of it, and have far less access to care. They are being raised by largely single parents who are working multiple jobs. They of course love their kids and do the best they can for them, but they are also often suffering from the effects of their own unprocessed trauma, on top of the onslaught of obstacles instigated by simply living in poverty. Without the resources and opportunities to work through trauma and other mental health challenges, many caregivers end up self-medicating, and if I'm being honest, I don't blame them.

I'm not condoning or recommending self-medication with drugs or alcohol; I'm just saying that when I see homeless people on the street, I think, "there but for the grace of God go I."[8] Had I been born into different circumstances, who's to say I wouldn't be an addict? I'm not proud of it, but I've self medicated with alcohol. I think most of us have, actually. At the end of a really long, hard day, or after an awful, triggering fight, most of us have—at one time or another (or many)—reached for a drink to calm our system. With an untreated mental illness, that feeling is the default. You can only bear it for so long. During those six months of waiting to change my prescription, most days I was anxious for hours on end despite my best efforts. If I don't have the option to take a nap or cry it out, and there's a drink in the fridge, I'll reach for it to make it stop for a while. Anything to make it stop.

Even with money, accessing professional services is rarely timely or simple. For my friends with depressive disorders, motivation and energy are particularly hard to come by. How is someone who can barely get out of bed and feed themself supposed to muster the mental stamina to investigate insurance policies, research providers, endure hideous waitlists, and keep appointments? On anxious days, I'm too paralyzed to answer phone calls, let alone make them. Add to that the demands of normal life: raising kids, performing at work, caring for aging parents, navigating complicated relationships, all the chores and bills and things that must be done. The odds of free time aligning with freedom from anxiety or depression can be ugly. And then there's the stigma that must be overcome to seek help.

PSYCHIATRY

When November finally limped its way to May, I had my first psychiatry appointment. Although I tried not to, I looked around at the other people sitting in the waiting room. My tribe sat there. I wondered at their stories and challenges, but not for very long, because my name was called.

My psychiatrist, Dr. Eckleburg, stood in her office doorway, from which she introduced herself with a smile, a handshake, and an invitation to take a seat opposite her at her desk. Kindly and professionally, she asked me routine questions about my history and symptoms from behind her computer screen where she entered my answers. I was grateful to answer many of her questions about things like suicide, abuse and eating disorders with "no." I don't take it for granted that I only have one diagnosis to bear; according to The National Alliance on Mental Illness, 60% of people with an anxiety disorder also have at least one other anxiety or depressive disorder to bear.[9]

After going through the obligatory questions, Dr. Eckleburg got to know me. I told her about our big relocation and my new manifestation of anxiety. I explained that I felt like I did before I ever started medication. She gave me options. We decided to keep me on the Wellbutrin and wean me off of my Effexor while simultaneously starting me on to a similar-yet-slightly-different antidepressant, Cymbalta. Then, she submitted my prescriptions, told me to schedule a follow-up at the front desk, and assured me that I could call her anytime if anything came up. I didn't have to wait until my next appointment. I was relieved to have the care available. It was all over in less than 20 minutes. It was a quick, relatively impersonal appointment, surprisingly unlike therapy. Unfortunately, my one-month transition from Effexor to Cymbalta would prove far more desperate than the six month wait that preceded it.

PART three

> Limping through the world,
> There's a knowing look or two,
> Is it just the cripples here
> Who understand the Truth?
>
> **REESE ROPER** *"SPARTAN" // FIVE IRON FRENZY*

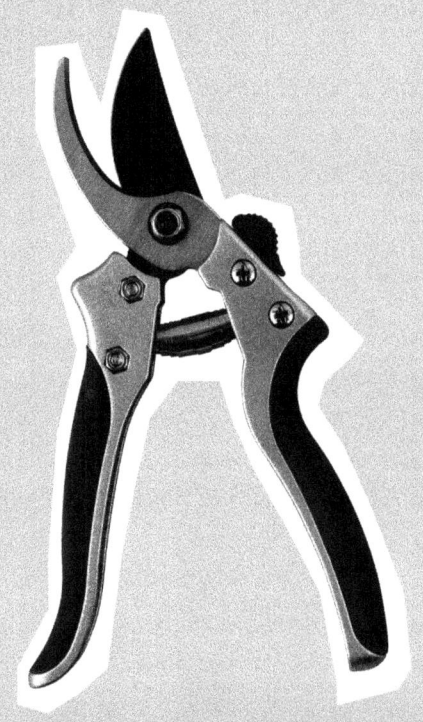

Pressing on

Chapter 9: Over Overcoming

In our backyard, we have some cacti that require pruning, so I know a thing or two about thorns. It makes me cringe to imagine living with one permanently piercing my skin. It would interfere with my daily life. With a thorn in my hand, I wouldn't be able to fully focus when writing. I'd have to modify my workouts and how I walk my dog. Hand-shaking would be awkward and likely embarrassing. It'd be hard to forget that my thorn is there. I'd pray to God to take it away, and then wonder why He didn't.

The Apostle Paul could relate. He described his weakness as a thorn. He shared with his friends in Corinth that he "implored the Lord three times that it might leave [him].[1] But it didn't, which is pretty relatable. To have an anxiety disorder is to have a thorn like Paul's. It has its ways of zapping energy, trashing plans, and injuring relationships. I want none of that, but it doesn't care.

Anxiety is a thorn that makes me weak. It disrupts the way I want to live. It impacts my productivity, my ability to relax, my social life, even my prayer life. And I pause to treat it. Boy, do I pause. I pray. I breathe meditatively. I do all that stuff I've told you about. I leave parties. I bust out my journal during church. I escape to bathroom stalls so I can focus on recovering sanity. I avoid phone calls. I keep to myself because I need to heal and

I don't want opportunities to be re-triggered. I collapse. On my bed. In tears. Before God.

Like this one day, during that one month when Dr. Eckleburg weaned me off of Effexor and onto Cymbalta. She cut the former dosage and replaced it with an equivalent dose of the latter. The goal was to eventually replace all of the Effexor with Cymbalta. In response to the change, my anxiety levels shot up.

It was during that difficult transitional month that Patrick and I got invited to a birthday party. It was a kid's party at a new friend's house, right after church. There was nothing particularly memorable about the church service that morning, but what happened afterward was. As Patrick and I ducked into his car, my muscles tensed, my heart skipped some beats, and my legs burned red. I sent out an SOS to Jesus: *Crap. It's coming. Help me!*

Patrick drove as I gazed out my open window, replaying the morning in search of a trigger for my anxiety. Nothing. I closed my eyes and tried again. Still, nothing. I was just on edge, without a reason why. I couldn't challenge a thought I couldn't find, so I tried attacking the anxiety on the physical front. I practiced 4-2-7 belly breathing and muscle exercises as I watched old suburbia float by. I felt better for moments, but those moments passed too quickly, so I broke the silence and said to Patrick, "Ugh, I'm having anxiety right now, and I don't know why."

"Okay. Did you do your journaling?"

"I can't, really, because I don't have an anxious thought. My body's just anxious. I'm just on edge. I tried my breathing and muscle relaxation, but the anxiety keeps coming back."

"Okay, so what do you want to do? Do you still want to go to the party?"

We were about to pass our street, so a decision had to be made. I was tired of letting anxiety call all the shots. I wanted to connect with people. Being new in town, I was hungry for friendship. Plus, sometimes I just need a distraction and some time for anxious adrenaline to finish working its way out of my body. I was hoping it would turn out to be one of those times.

"Let's go to the party," I said. "I'm tired of letting anxiety decide."

"Okay," Patrick nodded as we passed our street.

As we walked into our new friend's house, Patrick spotted a group of men and settled into conversation with them. I noticed a lot of familiar faces from church, but I couldn't find anyone I actually *knew*. No one from our small group was there. It felt like everyone had known each other forever. I felt like the anxious outsider, and having recently moved, I sort of *was*.

I hovered awkwardly over the food table in the backyard, eating too many pepperoni pizza slices and hoping for some conversation to distract me. I smiled and politely fake-laughed with people as they came and went. I tried to break through small talk into real talk. No luck, though.

So I tried another approach: When a couple acquaintances asked, "How are you?" I answered honestly: "Fine... a little anxious, though." But they just sort of nodded and faded away into other conversations that were more interesting, or at least more comfortable. All the while, my heart was still pounding, my throat constricted, my thoughts skittering, and breaths shallow.

I had to sit down.

The only empty chairs were at a table full of women from church whom I barely knew. I hesitated to join them, but took a leap of faith and sat down. No one acknowledged me. When I realized they were deep in conversation about breastfeeding and placenta, I wished I hadn't. As they shared battle stories about nipple infections, I did my best to look politely interested (but not creepy-interested). Mostly, though, I was tuning them out so I could count my breaths: inhale 1-2-3-4, hold 1-2, exhale

1-2-3-4-5-6-7. The breathing helped momentarily, but again, those moments passed too quickly.

I wanted to go home. I told Patrick. There must have been some miscommunication, though, because he didn't sense the urgency. We ended up staying another hour. My insides kept melting. It was a slow burn; that's almost always how it goes. I can function for quite a while during my typical anxiety attacks, but as the minutes turn to hours, it builds. On the rare occasions when I don't or can't deal with it, and enough time passes, I break down.

When Patrick and I were finally buckling our seat belts to go home, my eyes welled up. I cried because I was stuck, harassed by my own body, hijacked by my own brain. For two hours at that party, I was an outsider looking in. All I could do was feel my panic and my palpitations. Fellowship taunted me.

After a brief drive home, I swooped my journal off the coffee table, flew upstairs, and dove onto our bed where I let my tears run wild. Instantly, I collapsed at the feet of Jesus like so many desperate saints before me—crumpled, exhausted, and powerless.

My prayers were chest chokes, hyperventilation, bloodshot eyes, and clogged sinuses.

Patrick popped into the room.

"How can I help you, honey?"

"Can I have some hot mint tea?"

"Of course."

A few minutes later, he carefully handed me my steaming Snoopy mug. I took a sip and let the hot splash slow my breathing. That's always a good place to start. I told Alexa to shuffle my prayer playlist. Then I opened my journal. I'm usually not one to ask God, "Why?" but that afternoon, I did, in big cursive scribbles:

Why do I have to be the one at the party with the crazy insides?

Why must I stand by and listen to my arteries self-destruct?

I'm going to die early from this!

Why can't I just get over it?

Why can't I always live in the resurrection?

I guess this is some of the death —

For now, we carry both.

Why am I even anxious, anyway?

What I learned in therapy is futile now,

because my body's gonna do what it's gonna do.

It's been three intense hours. I'm supposed to feel better by now!

Will this ever end? Will I always feel like this?

So... defeated?

I am an utter failure. I let You down, God.

What good am I? Why can't I just get over this?

Is this my fault?

I broke down again, took another sip, and then let myself ask the scary question:

What if I lose my mind? What if I spiral into a state of insanity that robs me of my self? What if my personality crumbles and my skills melt and an institution awaits? Would it be my fault? Because I can't get over this?

And then God came near, because that's what He does for the "brokenhearted and crushed in spirit."[2] That Still Small Voice whispered the Truth:

Even if another diagnosis descends, even if my cognition changes, the most important part of me—the one at the core—will never change, because "He will never leave me nor forsake me."³ He will still speak to me in a way I will understand. God knows no boundaries. The Holy Spirit advocates to the Father on my behalf "with groanings that cannot be expressed in words."⁴

The Holy Spirit inspired me to scrawl this on the next page:

> Nothing can separate us from the love of God
> not psychosis
> nor panic attack
> nor bipolar disorder
> nor traumatic brain injury
> nor PTSD
> nor encephalitis
> nor any other awful result of the Fall.
> The Holy Spirit never leaves.
> God stays with us through it all.⁵

I opened my fists and turned my palms up in a gesture of offering, holding my anxiety and sanity loosely. Then I breathed out a prayer like the mother of God once did: "I am willing to be used of the Lord. Let it happen to me as you have said."⁶ And then He gave me rest. I fell into a nap. And when I woke up, I had peace of mind.

ORIGIN OF A THORN

In Jesus's Sermon on the Mount, He proclaimed, "Blessed are the weak in spirit." Well, "blessed" is not the first adjective that comes to mind when I think back on that day. "Weak" fits, though. I'm not saying Jesus was wrong, but to be honest, when I'm anxious, my weakness feels more like a curse than a blessing.

I'm not alone in this: the Apostle Paul felt a similar kind of way. In a letter to the church in Corinth, he described his weakness as "a thorn in the flesh, a messenger of Satan [given to] to torment [him]."⁷ He didn't call it a "blessing." At least not outright. I appreciate that Paul never specified what *kind* of thorn he had because his ambiguity leaves room for the full gamut of human pain: physical, mental, emotional, or relational. Whatever kind of thorn Paul had, it must have been bad. People don't refer to just anything as "a messenger of Satan sent to torment me."

It could be said that my thorn was sent from my genetics or life experience or brain chemicals or whatever, but ultimately, when I trace it to its root, I think "a messenger of Satan" isn't wrong. I know believing in Satan might sound basic, but have you seen the world? Have you felt the despair? Evil is real, and if I believe in a good Maker, I have to address the origin of the bad stuff, too.

Taken literally or figuratively, what scripture says makes sense to me: God created beings with free will, because if we didn't have a choice, reality wouldn't be so real and neither would Love. The story goes that an angel decided he'd rather be god than submit to the Real One, so he led a rebellion to overthrow All That Is Good. That rebellion is still under way. That angel, Satan, invited humanity into the drama by convincing the first humans to rebel against God as well. Human nature hasn't been the same since. We are beautiful beings created in the image of the Good Maker, but also, We All Ugly[8] because that nature has been corrupted, and with it, our relationship with our Incorruptible Maker.

All of this is to say that mental illness does not come from God. (It's also not a sin, but we'll save that for another chapter.) Rather, it is a thorn that comes from "a messenger of Satan," as Paul puts it. Thorns are spears hurled at God's beloved by Satan's rebellion. We all take hits; we all suffer, and those of us with faith in a good God ask Him for relief. Paul, for instance, "implored the Lord three times that [his thorn] might leave" him. But it didn't.

If healing were simply a matter of mustering up enough faith, then Paul of all people should have been able to remove his thorn. He was a highly educated religious leader, a notorious

"Pharisee of Pharisees" so committed to his religion that he persecuted Jesus's followers until a personal, miraculous encounter with the resurrected Jesus sent him down a completely different path.[9] Paul was changed from the inside out and given spiritual visions and revelations from God. A zealous apostle, he started church congregations all over the ancient Roman world at enormous cost, and then wrote poignant letters to advise and love those congregations from afar. Those letters now comprise much of the New Testament of the Bible. Paul suffered greatly for the Gospel: hunger and thirst and nakedness and shipwrecks and imprisonments and stoning and whippings a lash short of death.[10] In the midst of all that, Paul taught believers to "consider it all joy when you encounter trials of all kinds."[11] All this is to say that if anyone could pray the right prayer and believe the right things in order to remove his thorn, then Paul would have been the guy.

ON FAITH AND (NOT) HEALING

If the man who wrote much of the New Testament couldn't remove his thorn, then why should we expect anyone to be able remove theirs (or to manipulate God into doing it for them)? There is a false gospel that claims we should. It's called the Prosperity Gospel, and its proponents preach a promise of wealth, health, and power for God's faithful if they just embrace a passionate enough faith or send enough money to some master of healing. They tell us to "speak things into existence" and "name and claim" what we want in the name of the Lord.

The theology of the Prosperity Gospel is hell-bent on healing here and now. It overemphasizes glittery, self-serving, cherry-picked slices of scripture while ignoring the challenging call of Christ to die to ourselves and submit to the will of God. Without considering the complex, nuanced whole of scripture, select verses (like John 14:13 and Mt. 17:20) get manipulated by wolves in sheep's clothing to paint God as a doting genie whose powers are unlocked when we muster up the right combination of faith and emotion.

Then, when followers ask and don't receive, they are apt to blame themselves. That conclusion is extra damaging for anxious, perfectionism-prone people like myself. Can you imagine Paul encountering sermons and books with titles like "Remove Your Thorn!" "Pray Your Thorn Away!" or "Choose Christ, Not Your Thorn!"? What if Paul read them, did the things they told him to do, believed the things they told him to believe, but his thorn kept throbbing? Would he wonder, "Why does this work for everyone else, but not for me?" Would he feel like a broken failure? Would it cause him to spiral like I have?

That's what an oversimplified understanding of faith does to people like me and Paul, whom God, in His mysterious wisdom, chooses not to fully heal. Submitting our health, wealth, and future to God is easy if we believe that God simply has "plans to prosper us, not to harm us, to give us a hope and a future" here on Earth.[12] It's another story when we remember that Jesus said things like, "If they persecute me, they will persecute you also," "in this world you will have trouble," and "take up your cross and follow me."[13] When we consider that our Lord was the Suffering Servant, resolving to follow in His footsteps requires sincere trust and submission.[14] And I think that's sort of the point of all of this. God is far more interested in the quality of my soul, "of the nearness of my heart to His,"[15] than He is in the ease of my life—a vapor in light of eternity[16].

CONTENT WITH DISTRESSES

Just because Paul's thorn wasn't removed doesn't mean his prayer wasn't answered. He perceived a response from God, which he shared in his letter to the church in Corinth. Right after describing his pain and his prayers about it, he writes this:

> And [God] has said to me, 'My grace is sufficient for you, for My power is perfected in weakness.' Most gladly, therefore, I will rather boast about my weaknesses, so that the power of Christ may dwell in me. Therefore I am well content

with weaknesses, with insults, with distresses, with persecutions, with difficulties, for Christ's sake; for when I am weak, then I am strong.

I can't speak to insults or persecutions, but I can relate to the weaknesses and distresses. To be "well content with distress" is quite a paradox, but I think I get it. I think that's where I landed on that Sunday afternoon when I laid on my bed and surrendered my sanity to God. While I was distressed to tears, on a deeper spiritual level, once I surrendered my sanity to God, I was at peace with bearing my thorn because—in short—Jesus had taught me to trust him with my sanity.

Don't get me wrong, I don't think that God delights in my suffering or anyone else's. Good parents don't delight in their kids' tears over going to the dentist. It pains them to see their kids in distress. But good parents know what's best in the big picture. I know it's more complicated than that, but I think the principle applies: God does not delight in my suffering, but He sees a bigger picture that I can't fathom. On one hand, He longs to heal me, but on the other, He knows my temporary suffering is for the Mysterious Good of All Things. Heaven will be more full. I will become more like Jesus. Others will be helped. Something like that. Something like what Paul wrote to the church in Rome:

> Suffering produces perseverance; perseverance, character; and character, hope. And this hope will not lead to disappointment. For we know how dearly God loves us, because he has given us the Holy Spirit to fill our hearts with his love.[17]

I trust that He is crafting a beautiful story from the darkness that He is constantly redeeming—a huge story that interweaves your complex story with mine and a million others' and stretches into eternity—one He gives us glimpses into every now and then. One day, we'll celebrate it in its fullness on the other side of eternity. It's like the lyrics to this Five Iron Frenzy song, "The Greatest Story Ever Told":

All my dreams are slowly dying
I can count my years in scars

The only One that's never left me
Has carried me so very far
I've heard it said that He wastes nothing,
So beautiful to behold
The Author of my hope is writing
The greatest story ever told

JESUS'S THORN

We who suffer are not alone: God has endured profound suffering through the life and death of Jesus Christ, who not only changed eternity, but modeled how to suffer well. Jesus's most passionate prayer, the night before his death, was not about making his desires become his reality; on the contrary, it was about putting his desires aside and being faithful. Hours before Jesus was arrested and crucified, he prayed in the Garden of Gethsemane. His friend and disciple, Mark, recalled the somber night like this:

> [We] went to a place called Gethsemane, and Jesus said to [us], 'Sit here while I pray.' He took Peter, James and John along with him, and he began to be deeply distressed and troubled. 'My soul is overwhelmed with sorrow to the point of death,' he said to them. 'Stay here and keep watch.' Going a little farther, he fell to the ground and prayed that if possible the hour might pass from him. 'Abba, Father,' he said, 'everything is possible for you. Take this cup from me. Yet not what I will, but what you will.'[18]

God responded when "an angel from heaven appeared to him and strengthened him." Then Jesus prayed it all over again, which is so human, and so divine.[19] Surely, Jesus had enough faith when he asked God, "that if possible, the hour might pass from [Me]," and surely, Jesus was sincere when he pleaded with his Father to "take this cup from Me." He was desperate to avoid the whip, the nails, the betrayal, the heartbreak, the nakedness, the suffocation, the death... who wouldn't be? Mostly, He was desperate for another way to deal with humanity's problem of sin. Yet, he had to take it all on: he was the only one who could drink from that cup because he was the only one with no sin of his own. He knew it would tear a new rip in eternity, temporarily separating him from the Triune God. The divine anguish was heard in Jesus's final cry on the cross: "My God, my God, why have you forsaken me?"[20]

Jesus didn't get the answer he longed for—another way to deal with humanity's problem of sin—that night in Gethsemane. Surely, it wasn't his fault that his Father didn't acquiesce. Surely, his faith didn't fall short. On the contrary, Jesus's prayer in Gethsemane, like all of His prayers, serves as a model for His disciples. In Gethsemane, He teaches us to pour out our deepest anxieties and desires to God, to emote fully before the one who made us. And then instead of fixating on getting what we want, He teaches us to surrender our will to God's better one in saying, "yet not what I will, but what You will."

Ultimately, Jesus chose to submit and endure the cross and all its anxiety "for the joy set before him": the glorious reunion of God with His beloved children.[21] Jesus's suffering was anything but pointless. The same is true of yours and mine.

Chapter 10: Redemption: The Power of Weakness

A couple months after my psychiatrist, Dr. Eckleburg, changed my medication, when my body had had enough time to adjust to my new full dose of Cymbalta, my anxiety became manageable again. I entered a new season of relief.

It was during this time that on a sunny San Diego day, as I was driving to the grocery store, my mind wandered into what-if scenarios of international, near-apocalyptic proportions. Inspired by the morning's regularly terrifying headlines, I imagined a nuclear attack and takeover of the US by China or Russia or some evil hybrid of the two. In place of the green lawns and exotic flowers I drove past, I saw dirt and rubble. Instead of happy families riding bikes, I saw foreign soldiers patrolling ashy remains. I saw hunger, tears, everything dreary. Naturally, this made me anxious.

I know a lot of people get plagued by intrusive thoughts like those, especially nowadays. It used to be that we read a limited number of heavy headlines once a day in the newspaper, but now we are free to drown ourselves in updates as we doom scroll our way to bedtime. It can quickly and easily become too much information, especially when it's terrible stuff we have no control over. What results is a sort of doom-and-gloom anxiety that is not exclusive to people who suffer from clinical disorders.

It is (unfortunately) available to all of us! I have found a passage by C.S. Lewis to be of great comfort in this regard. While Lewis came long before the internet, he did live in an anxious age: England during WWII. It was a time of common death, air raids, genocide, and high anxiety. In an essay titled, "On Living in an Atomic Age," Lewis urged people to live in the present rather than the always-uncertain future. I come back to it when fear of the future seeps into my system, like it did that sunny morning as I drove to the grocery store.

> 'How are we to live in an atomic age?' I am tempted to reply: 'Why, as you would have lived in the sixteenth century when the plague visited London almost every year, or as you would have lived in a Viking age when raiders from Scandinavia might land and cut your throat any night; or indeed, as you are already living in an age of cancer, an age of syphilis, an age of paralysis, an age of air raids, an age of railway accidents, an age of motor accidents.'
>
> In other words, do not let us begin by exaggerating the novelty of our situation. Believe me, dear sir or madam, you and all whom you love were already sentenced to death before the atomic bomb was invented...
>
> This is the first point to be made: and the first action to be taken is to pull ourselves together. If we are all going to be destroyed by an atomic bomb, let that bomb when it comes find us doing sensible and human things—praying, working, teaching, reading, listening to music, bathing the children, playing tennis, chatting to our friends over a pint and a game of darts—not huddled together like frightened sheep and thinking about bombs. They may break our bodies but they need not dominate our minds.[1]

That passage laid a path for a new stream of thoughts that morning as I drove through my imagined war-zone. It wasn't just Lewis, however, who inspired me to ask the question that followed. It was probably also part Holy Spirit, part recently-surrendering-my-sanity-to-Jesus, and part friends-and-pastors-who-ask-great-questions. Whatever inspired the question, I am grateful it settled into my soul:

Why am I so disturbed by these thoughts? What is being threatened?

At the next stoplight, I answered my self: *Well, a national takeover like that would shatter my life, my happiness, my dreams.*

Really? What does that say about where I'm at spiritually?

Maybe it says that I've built my house on sand.[2]

Then the counselor in my brain asked, *What would still be True if my free country gets taken over by an evil dictatorship?* I thought back to that day I laid on my bed with my tears and my mint tea.

The same things that would still be true if I lost my sanity:
God would still be in control.
God would still love me.
God would still be that "friend who sticks closer than a brother."[3]
God would still understand what I'm going through.
He would still miraculously be Enough.

There would certainly be more heartbreak, grief, lament, and struggle. But Jesus, who is called "a man of sorrows, acquainted with grief," would understand entirely.[4] He wouldn't leave my side. He would listen when I cried out. He would let me question him and pound on his chest. He could take it. He gets us: "For we do not have a high priest who is unable to empathize with our weaknesses, but we have one who has been tempted in every way, just as we are—yet He did not sin."[5] No matter our societal or political circumstances, those core Truths will never change.

As I rounded the corner to Smart and Final, the anxiety subsided. Apparently, holding my sanity with open hands was good practice for holding the future of the free world with open hands. I suppose this is what C.S. Lewis meant in *Mere Christianity*, where he wrote about "learning your driving in a hard school." It was the first literary passage to make me feel seen as a Christian with an anxiety disorder:

> If you are a poor creature, poisoned by a wretched up-bringing in some house full of vulgar jealousies and senseless quarrels—saddled, by no choice of your own, with some loathsome sexual perversion [or Bipolar Disorder, or Schizophrenia, or Panic Disorder, or Major Depressive Disorder, or OCD, or GAD]—nagged day in and day out by an inferiority complex that makes you snap at your best friends—do not despair. He knows all about it. You are one of the poor whom He blessed. He knows what a wretched machine you are trying to drive. Keep on. Do what you can. One day (perhaps in another world, but perhaps far sooner than that), He will fling it on the scrap-heap and give you a new one. And then you may astonish us all – not least yourself: for you have learned your driving in a hard school.

"Poisoned," "saddled," and "nagged" sound a lot like mental illness to me. My disorder poisons the Truth, saddles me with physical exhaustion, and nags at me with lies and discomfort. Just as horses have no say in getting saddled; neither does anyone ultimately get to decide how emotionally, mentally, or physically well they get to be, or for how long. There is a lot we can do to tip the odds in our favor—things like mindfulness, exercising, and eating well—but nature and nurture are always capable of turning the tables. Each of us is dealt genetics, circumstances, family, and trauma that we do not get to choose. We simply get what we get: some of us get new Lexuses, and some of us get lemons that break down all the time and require a ton of maintenance. The miracle of it all is that when we invite God into our lemon ordeals, we tend to grow in ways that Lexus owners seldom do.

PROTECTION FROM PRIDE

The Apostle Paul had a lemon, except he didn't know about lemon laws or cars, so he called his a thorn. After lamenting the suffering it caused him, he did something crazy. He *welcomed* it. He saw God's purpose for it, and he shared about it in a letter to the church he started in Corinth:

> Because of the surpassing greatness of the [spiritual] revelations [given to me], for this reason, to keep me from exalting myself, there was given me a thorn in the flesh.

In other words, along with his thorn, Paul was given profound spiritual Truths and experiences to share with the Early Church. As an apostle, he performed signs and miracles that lent credibility to his message. Given his spiritual resume, it would have been easy for Paul to feel like a pretty big deal—being chosen by God to receive visions and dreams and followers. Gifts like that can easily lead to self-conceit because it is so easy to forget that gifts are just that—given, not earned. We are not their ultimate source; there is only one Giver of Gifts. To forget that is to open ourselves to conceit and sinful pride. As the proverb says, "Pride comes before destruction, and an arrogant spirit before a fall."[6] In terms of spiritual health, it's safer to be weak than strong.

I like how C.S. Lewis puts it in *Mere Christianity*: "Much is expected from those to whom much is given. If you mistake for your own merits what are really God's gifts to you through nature... all those gifts will only make your fall more terrible."

The thing about Paul, though, is that he didn't have a "terrible fall." He didn't spend parishioner's hard-earned money to wrap himself in luxury or get caught up in scandalous affairs or forget Jesus while bathing in the spotlight. Despite the great works God accomplished through him, Paul couldn't buy into the lie that he was high and mighty because his thorn continually brought him to his knees. Its throbbing wouldn't let him forget;

it kept him returning to his Savior in desperate need. His thorn was a persistent reminder of where his strength came from, and it prevented him from taking credit for the good works God did through him. Ultimately, in the Kingdom of God, it might be said that God let Paul's thorn remain to protect him from himself, not to mention those under his influence and care.

Like Paul without his thorn, without GAD, I would quite likely be some sort of spiritual disaster, "mistaking for my own merits what are really God's gifts to me." The story God's been writing in my life has been a generous one, marked by opportunities for spiritual growth, deep fellowship, and great spiritual role models, both ones I've known personally and ones whose art has influenced me profoundly from afar. I'm no apostle or spiritual superstar, but like Paul, my faith story features privileged experiences that tempt me toward pride, so I decided to write my own version of his passage. I ended up with this:

Because of the *fact that I grew up in the Church, have been in relationship with Jesus since 7th grade or so, have been on mission trips in five countries, have been a Young Life volunteer for 20 years, have a Master's degree and financial security, and because He's blessed me with this enduring intimacy with Him,* for this reason, to keep me from exalting myself, there was given me a thorn in my flesh *called Generalized Anxiety Disorder,* a messenger of Satan sent to torment me—to keep me from exalting myself! Concerning this I implored the Lord *28,459,084* times that it might leave me. And He has said to me, 'My grace is sufficient for you, for My power is perfected in weakness.' Most gladly, therefore, I will rather boast about my weaknesses, so that the power of Christ may dwell in me. Therefore I am *sometimes* well content with weaknesses, ~~with insults~~, with distresses, ~~with persecutions~~, with difficulties, for Christ's sake; for when I am weak, then I am strong.

I can't claim all of Paul's words, so I crossed some out. I haven't been insulted enough or persecuted ever, so I'd be a fool to claim contentment with either. If these pages land in enough hands, though, I'll probably get a lot of practice with the insult part on Twitter or "X" or whatever it's called when this is finally published. I'll keep you posted.

BECOMING INTERRUPTIBLE

Not only do thorns encourage humility; they also cause inconvenience. Anxiety attacks don't empower me to cross more items off my to-do list. They don't help me to "do more for God." However, they do help me become more like Jesus, and isn't that always the point?

Jesus didn't live at a frazzled pace, trying to do more, more, more for His Father. He didn't get upset with the needy people who interrupted Him in the middle of his sermons and journeys. He embraced them as part of the ever-unfolding will of God for His life. He embodied Proverbs 16:9: "In their hearts humans plan their course, but the Lord establishes their steps." Jesus always had a plan, a direction He was headed in, but He held it loosely, leaving space for His Father to redirect His steps. When Jesus was interrupted by desperate people, sacred moments happened: the kinds that multiple witnesses recorded, the kinds worth talking about more than 2000 years later. When anxiety interrupts my plans, may I remember that I, too, can trust the One who is directing my steps.

It's hard, though. The growth is slow and bumpy. It doesn't take long for my open hands to close into tight fists that treat needy people like obstacles rather than the dignified sisters and brothers they are. It's all too easy for me to treat God's plan as a hindrance to mine. And this is where my thorn blesses me: without giving me a choice, it trains me to live an interruptible life at the pace God sets, rather than the frantic one I get tempted to shove my minutes through. Because I have learned to bend my plans for anxiety attacks, I have become more apt to bend them for others like Jesus did.

RECOGNIZING NEED

Here in American suburbia, from where I write these words, it's easy to assume that I can skip the part of the Lord's prayer that says, "Give us this day, our daily bread," because I am fully capable of getting my own bread, thank you very much. But ultimately, it's not up to me. It's because I live in this country, at this time, under this government, with this climate, with the right opportunities and privileges that I can work (or at this moment, collect unemployment) for money to buy plenty of bread. I can even stock-pile it.

And it all feels like self-sufficiency. But remove some of those circumstances, and it becomes clear that my ability to get bread is beyond me. It is from God, who orchestrates all factors—economic, environmental, agricultural, political, and all the other -icals required to bless me with bread, and it's He who planted me when and where I am, rather than in some other context, like Ireland's Great Potato Famine or Ukraine's tragic present. The poor in spirit whom Jesus blessed need not be poor in physical resources, although in the upside-down kingdom, it certainly helps. I think they are simply those who approach life from an awareness of their reliance on God as their Provider and Sustainer.

I think Jesus sort of had this in mind when He said, "It is easier for a camel to enter the eye of a needle than for a rich person to enter the kingdom of God." (Thankfully, He followed that with, "but with God, all things are possible.") Jesus didn't say that because He's anti-rich-people, but because entering the kingdom of God requires acknowledging our need and inviting Christ to fill it. In fact, Jesus's elaboration on "blessed are the poor (in spirit)" is "for they shall receive the kingdom of heaven." In other words, the wealthy—be it physically, mentally, emotionally, or socially—struggle to receive the things of God because they struggle to see their need for Him. Deep spiritual need easily gets buried and forgotten beneath layers of achievement and comfort. Out of sight, out of mind.

The reality is that despite our awareness, we're all in need of a relationship with the One who made us. That's what we were made for. The problem is that God is perfect and "we all have sinned and fallen short of the glory of God."[7] We can never work our way to Perfection, which means we can never work our way to God. We will always be fighting that little devil on our shoulder, and even if we rarely act on his demands, we often welcome his thoughts, the ones that dehumanize, judge, lust, and hate. This is where we must admit need. Having other needs—be they physical, mental, or emotional—helps set the stage to recognize spiritual needs, too.

Thanks to God's redemptive work through my thorn, I have been learning to better recognize my ongoing need for Jesus. Although I decided long ago to follow Jesus, I still really need His help, which is actually a beautiful thing because it means I get to be helped by God. I love this ancient picture of what that looks like:

> There is no one like the God of Israel,
> who rides through the skies to help you,
> who rides on the clouds in His majesty.
> The everlasting God is your place of safety,
> and His arms will hold you up forever.[8]

It's not about being strong, it's about being loved by the One who helps me in my weakness. It's about God's belief that I'm worth His time, worth "riding through the skies and on the clouds" for. There's a sacred dignity in collapsing before God. Jesus did it. So did David and Elijah and Hagar and Moses and a million other saints.[9] And this is why it's good to have a thorn. It pokes holes in "my" strength, which reminds me that beneath all my achievements, my money, my people, and my status, that I am a beloved daughter of a God who saves me from my thoughts, despair, and sin. He saves me from the monster I become when I get judgemental and self-absorbed. He reminds me that I am not my own savior, let alone anyone else's, which is actually quite a relief. In this way, it is a blessing to have a thorn. It opens my eyes to my need; if it went unseen, I might never open my hands to receive.

Chapter 11: Speaking of Stigma

It's been twenty-two years since I sat through my most memorable sermon. I told you about it all the way back in chapter two, which was a long time ago. I'm sorry about that, but I'm a new author, and so you're just going to have to put up with this awkward transition back to it. It's that sermon preached by Pastor Calihan in my hometown at Oak Hills Church. I was 19. If you're an Elder Millennial like me who grew up in 90's Evangelical culture, chances are you've heard some version of it, too. The loudest part went like this:

> Scripture is the only weapon needed by the faithful believer to win the fight against depression and anxiety! Believers shouldn't be going to worldly sources like therapy and medication! Anxiety and depression are spiritual ailments that need spiritual remedies! Scripture alone is enough, and if it isn't, then you need more faith!

It's taken a couple of decades to process where that message came from and why it was preached. I finally have some sort of idea that's hopefully worth sharing. Because, well, I'm sharing it.

ANXIOUS ABOUT ANTIDEPRESSANTS

That sermon was delivered back in 2002 when, for the first time, society's talk of anxiety disorders, depressive disorders, and antidepressants became loud enough to concern my local church. In this regard, it was actually a timely (although unhealthy) message. According to *The New York Times*,

> In 1988, a year after the Food and Drug Administration approved Prozac, 2,469,000 prescriptions for it were dispensed in America. By 2002, that number had risen to 33,320,000. By 2008, antidepressants were the third-most-common prescription drug taken in America.

Suffice it to say that in the 1990's-2000's, the Church in America witnessed a dramatic proliferation of antidepressant use. It is no wonder that pastors and church leaders expressed skepticism, concern, and even fear. I don't entirely blame them. Whereas antidepressants have only been around for a matter of decades, religion and spirituality have been humanity's go-to for inner-healing for millennia. Suddenly, psychiatry was encroaching on religion's turf. Leaders like Pastor Calihan feared that their people would give up the difficult work of soul-searching, prayer, scripture study, accountability, and wise counsel for the newer, far-easier alternative: antidepressants. They feared that doctors were writing prescriptions to rid people of the unpleasant emotions and struggles that are common to humanity—the very emotions and circumstances that God uses to draw people to Himself.

I imagine faith leaders fearing a future like the one Aldous Huxley painted in his dystopian novel, *Brave New World*: a world where people line up to pop pills that dull their emotions and distance them from reality so that they can enjoy lighter, easier existences. And honestly, that's not very far of a stretch. Way before antidepressants, we already had plenty of options for avoiding pain. They're the same healthy and harmful options that we have today: alcohol, drugs, entertainment, work, sex, hobbies, relationships, volunteering—anything—to distract us from the painful realities festering within us.

Knowing humanity's proclivity for escapism, pastors' concerns about antidepressants were, to an extent, warranted. Scripture charges leaders to protect the spiritual health of those who have been given to them, and since antidepressants alter mental and emotional health, they alter spiritual health, too. The writer of Acts advised the leaders of the Early Church to "be on guard for yourselves and for all the flock, among which the Holy Spirit has made you overseers, to shepherd the Church of God which He purchased with His own blood." The writer then continues, warning that "savage wolves will come in among you, not sparing the flock."[1] And that's what leaders like mine thought they were doing—protecting their people from this new "savage wolf" that was out to stunt its victims' spiritual growth.

Perhaps pastors were concerned that medicating thorns would prevent their people from receiving their redemptive spiritual benefits. C.S. Lewis alludes to these benefits in his book, *The Problem of Pain*:

> God whispers to us in our pleasures, speaks in our conscience, but shouts in our pains: it is his megaphone to rouse a deaf world.

Anyone with faith the size of a mustard seed will plead with a higher power when they or their loved ones' health or wellbeing is threatened. Worry is capable of bringing distant believers back to prayer and tempting atheists to hope in Providence. If C.S. Lewis is right about the spiritual power of pain, then wouldn't taking "happy pills" be like shushing the Spirit? Plenty of people would rather seek a prescription than seek God.

In this regard, I understand why people of faith might not only give medication serious side-eye, but straight-on glares. Unfortunately, those glares deeply affect the minority of us who benefit not only mentally and emotionally—but also spiritually—from antidepressants.

THE THINGS PEOPLE SAY

I kept my anxiety disorder a secret from almost everyone in my life for nearly a decade following my diagnosis in 2007. Patrick knew, of course, and so did Annie, a colleague-turned-friend. Annie is a young, energetic Spanish teacher who openly spoke about her Bipolar Disorder. We were enjoying margaritas after work one day when she mentioned her medication journey. As vulnerability breeds vulnerability, I told her about mine. A few weeks later in the staff lounge, I gave her an update:

"So, my new prescription is working, and I'm in a good place!"

"Wow, that's soooo good!" she said. "If it helps you, then stay on it! Forever! Seriously! I mean that!"

Unfortunately, not everyone celebrates healing like Annie because not everyone understands mental illness like she does. Many people, especially Christians in my experience, fail to understand that anxiety *disorders* are markedly different from the kind of anxiety that everyone struggles with from time to time. Because their anxiety often has spiritual roots related to trusting or surrendering to God, they offer spiritual solutions and "encouragement" with kind intentions but devastating effects for those of us who are suffering clinically. I have been both witness to and recipient of Bible verse band-aids and spiritual tips too many times to recall.

When those conversations happen, they remind me of my senior year of high school when I cried in front of my pre-calc teacher, Mrs. Krem. She was a no-nonsense, middle-aged math teacher with shoulder-length graying hair and a stern face. I was desperate to transfer to a lower level of math, and so on the last day to change classes, I stopped by her room to get her signature for approval. The conversation went like this:

"Hi, Mrs. Krem. I need to drop this class. Would you please sign this form for me?"

She stood up from her desk, and asked in monotone, "Why do you need to drop?"

"I'm failing... I'm having a really hard time understanding the material."

Her eyebrows raised slightly. "Well, are you doing the homework?"

"Yes."

"Are you paying attention and taking notes during class?"

"Yes."

"Are you participating in the group work?"

"Yes."

"So... why don't you get it?" And that's when I cried because clearly, there was something wrong with me, and also, so much for college.

Many Christian leaders and authors use crappy checklists like Mrs. Krem's to "help" people like me who struggle with mental health. The anxiety checklist goes like this:

"Are you presenting your requests to God in a spirit of thanks?"

"Have you truly surrendered your future to the Lord?"

"Have you applied these scriptures and read these books?"

"Then why are you still anxious?" Which is to say that my anxiety is all my fault and that I am a broken human being.

Jesus's disciples pulled this kind of narrow-minded thinking, too. They pointed out a blind man and asked Jesus, "Rabbi, who sinned, this man or his parents, that he was born blind?" (What stigma and shame he must have endured!)

Jesus set them straight: "Neither this man nor his parents sinned, but this happened so that the works of God might be displayed in him."[2] Jesus cured the man, and the rest of the story is pretty great, but the point is this: It is wrong to assume that hard things like blindness, anxiety disorders, and math allergies are the result of anyone's personal sins.

All of these interactions were unhelpful and ineffective because assumptions were made. My math teacher assumed that my brain worked like hers, the disciples assumed disabilities were punishments, and too many Christians assume that everyone's anxiety is the same.

I doubt that Mrs. Krem, the disciples, and mentally healthy people want to be insensitive and hurtful, so to provide a little insight, what follows are a few real conversations I've had that illustrate what is helpful and what is hurtful to people with disorders who are brave enough to talk about them.

GEORGE: TESTIMONIALS

In case you're unaware, high school teachers never have time for anything. We actually have negative time, which doesn't work out so well for cognitive journaling and the like. We get five minutes between classes to do all the things: nudging slow kids out of our classrooms, peeing, getting coffee, making copies, filling our water bottles and repelling students who try to hand us random papers in hallways.

During one of those breaks, my colleague, George, fresh off his prep period, saw me in my classroom and popped in. As much as I wanted to listen to what went down in his fourth period, I just couldn't because I had been stuck in an anxiety whirlpool for the last 45 minutes, and I only had five minutes to try and climb out of it. So when he asked, "How's it going?" I answered honestly in hopes that he might take the hint.

"I'm okay, but a little anxious."

"Oooh, you get anxious? You know what?! You should stop eating gluten! I'm like a new man since I cut it out! Oh, and you know what else?! Have you read such-and-such self-help book? You *MUST*. It totally changed the way I think! I'm now anxiety-free—"

"Okay, great, I'll look into those!" (No I won't.)

I headed to the door to lose him in the hallway and pursue solitude in the one place on campus it's guaranteed: the bathroom.

I know George was trying to help, but this is what I wished he realized: when someone is splashing at the surface, gasping for air, you don't tell them about options for local swim lessons. You don't inspire them with stories of your swim-team glory days. Assuming anyone's anxiety is the same as yours, either in cause or experience, is never a good idea. Anxiety and brains aren't aren't made in Henry Ford's factory. Please stop simplifying the situation. We are each uniquely complex. Rather than making it about your story, jump into my current one by asking, "What can I do to help you?"

I'm not saying that it's pointless to share our stories and strategies—after all, that's what I'm doing here—but that day at work, I just needed some quiet so I could journal. George mistakenly assumed that his solution must be my solution. If he had only asked, "What usually helps you when you're anxious?" I could have told him, and he could have left me alone to do it. Then, after school the next day, he could have asked me about my anxiety journey and then shared his, and it would have been meaningful.

DAISY: BIBLE VERSE BAND-AIDES

Sunday mornings are prime time for awkward anxiety conversations like this one. It started right when church got out. At some point during the sermon, my anxiety got triggered, but I couldn't pinpoint why or how. I had no anxious thoughts, but I did have a pounding heart, short breath, and an inability to think straight. I was just trying to make it to my car without small talk so I could do some deep breathing.

From a few steps behind, someone said, "Hey, Tiffany!"

I turned around. "Hi, Daisy."

"How are you?" she cheerily asked.

"I'm okay, thanks!"

I left it at that because I didn't want to get into it. I just wanted to melt down in the privacy of my car. A moment later, though, I decided to practice what I preach and be vulnerable. So I added, "I'm feeling kind of anxious, though."

"Oh. That's a bummer. When I'm anxious about something, it helps me to remember that Bible verse, 'Be anxious for nothing, but pray about everything.'"[3]

This is to say that I apparently don't trust God enough or pray well enough. Once again, I am reminded that my own faith community misunderstands me. But because I'm near panic mode, I choose flight over fight and say, "Yeah, thanks. Bye!"

By that point, though, I already feel worse. I am reminded of what a horrible failure I am. My heart pounds a little harder, my chest and face flush a little redder, and I beeline it to my car where I finally let the tears leak out.

I'm anxious again and it's all my fault. I should "be anxious for nothing," but here I am, being what I shouldn't be. I don't know how to stop this. Maybe if I... just read my Bible more, just pray with more faith, just "trust God" more, just read the right inspirational Christian books, just listen to the "right" music, just get more in tune with His will, just study theology more rigorously... ....maybe if I just didn't fail so much, ... then I wouldn't be so anxious. This. Is. All. My. Fault.

I know Daisy didn't want to make me cry. I know she had good intentions. But much like the people who ask those crappy checklist questions, she was operating out of the assumption that my kind of anxiety was the same as hers, which was pretty lame of her because she knew I have an anxiety disorder.

Clearly, though, she didn't understand GAD. Many people don't know the desperate darkness of mental illness. For their sake, I'm glad they haven't had to experience it. But because their experience is limited, and because they don't ask and therefore don't listen, they assume that depressive disorders are the same as their own struggles with discontentment and laziness, and that anxiety disorders are the same as their own struggles to trust God with their present and future.[4] They feed us verses like "Rejoice always!" and "Do not worry about tomorrow," and say things like, "I used to get anxious too, but then I learned to give it to the Lord, and now I don't anymore!" They confuse their spiritual struggles with our mental illness symptoms and end up hurting us more than helping us.

I wish Daisy would have remembered this Bible verse instead: "Be quick to listen and slow to speak." I wish she would have asked me about my anxiety before tossing a scripture band-aid at it (which landed in a sensitive spot). I want her to know that when I'm anxious, "be anxious for nothing" just makes me feel like that much more of a failure. I want her to acknowledge that there are different kinds of anxiety that deserve different responses. Before doling out advice or suggestions, terms must be defined, roots must be explored, and discernment must be applied if we are to help, rather than hurt, one another. That's a tall order for anyone who isn't a counselor, therapist, or pastor though, and so it is up to pastors, elders, and leaders within the Church to teach their flocks how to support their brothers and sisters with mental illness.

The injuries inflicted on me by many well-meaning Daisys and Georges kept me silent about my anxiety for nearly a decade. With the exception of Patrick, I told no one when I was feeling anxious. It risked too much. When anxiety struck at work or church, I headed to a bathroom stall to work through my thoughts without the risk of having to explain myself.

VALENTINA: HOW TO NOT PUNCH PEOPLE

One of the redeeming aspects of being treated for a disorder is that over time, you learn how to help others who suffer similarly. This has come in handy many times in my work as a teacher.

For example, when I was working at a continuation school, one of my students, Valentina, refused to come back inside from lunch. Valentina was an intelligent, sassy, 17 year-old Latina in my English class. It's not out of character for her to socialize past the tardy bell, but this time, she was pacing back and forth on the blacktop *alone*. I had a co-teacher inside, so I stepped out and approached her.

"Hey, Val, are you coming inside?"

She kept pacing and didn't acknowledge me. Her eyes were fuming through her thick eyeliner. I tried again. "Val, What's going on? Are you okay?"

"Ms. Ciccone, I can't go in there right now! I have too much anxiety! Like, if I go in there, I'm going to punch someone, I swear to God! And I don't wanna get in trouble!" Her wide eyes and sharp movements told me she meant it.

"Did something happen?"

"No! Sometimes my anxiety just comes out of nowhere! I can't even help it!" I know exactly what she means.

"Do you remember what was going on when the anxiety started?"

She paused for a minute, and then, "Oohhh yeaaah! I heard someone talking about my ex, and..." She trailed off and continued the conversation in her head.

I gave her a minute, and then asked, "Do you want to talk about it?"

"Nah." Her eyes softened a little, but she was still keyed-up and restless.

"Ok, yeah, that's fine, you don't need to talk to me about it... So what usually helps you when you feel anxious like this?"

"Usually, I like, punch stuff." I imagine where I could hang a punching bag in my classroom. She's not the only student who could use one.

"Well, unfortunately, that's not really an option right now, but I know what you mean. Sometimes, our bodies just need to get the adrenaline out. Something that helps me is to go for a fast walk. Would you be open to trying that with me now?"

"Yeah, ok."

"Ok, let me go in and tell Ms. Hernandez we're going."

We power walked the campus for 15 minutes. I made her keep up with my pace while asking her about the help she's getting for her anxiety. I shared some of my story and tried to encourage her. When we got back to the door, I asked, "How do you feel now?"

"Better." So did I.

"Good enough to go inside?"

"Yeah." We walked in together and got back to work.

If it weren't for my first-hand experience with anxiety and therapy, I wouldn't have known what to do with Valentina. I might have misinterpreted her behavior as defiance and doled out consequences accordingly, which would have further fueled her rage against me and the system I worked for. I wouldn't be surprised if her anxiety played a major role in landing her in continuation school in the first place.

For the sake of helping people like Valentina and myself, and for empowering people like Daisy and George who want to help but don't know how, here is a series of questions that I ask, both of myself and others like Valentina, when we struggle.

"WHAT USUALLY HELPS YOU WHEN YOU'RE FEELING ANXIOUS?"

When I am on the receiving end of this question, it helps me recall my tools and strategies and subtly encourages me to use them. Sometimes, I really need that encouragement because my anxious thoughts try to prevent me from taking action against them. For example, right now, as I'm typing this, I'm anxious. It started about 20 minutes ago. I know journaling will help, but have I done it? No! Instead, I'm listening to my anxiety's trash talk:

I'll never finish writing this section! I'm going nowhere. I have to do this now, or it will never be done! This shouldn't be taking me so long! I don't really need to journal—this will probably just go away on its own!

If you were here now, sitting across the table from me and asked, "What usually helps you when you're anxious?" I would answer, "cognitive journaling," which would encourage me to open my journaling document and actually do it. Then, I would probably start feeling better. Now, excuse me while I type in that doc for a while.

Okay, I'm back. When I asked Valentina what usually helps her when she's anxious," she answered, "I don't know. I usually punch stuff." You might get an answer like that, so it helps to have some simple suggestions on hand. Here are a few:

GUIDE THEM THROUGH A BREATHING EXERCISE.

When stressed or anxious, I default to 4-2-7 belly breathing Others prefer box breathing (4-4-4) or other forms of belly breathing. You can find and save guided videos on YouTube for all kinds of breathing and meditation exercises, and then play them as needed for an anxious friend or your anxious self.

SUGGEST PHYSICAL EXERCISE.

Intense anxiety like Valentina's needs to work itself out of the body, which is probably why she finds punching—mattresses and pillows, I ignorantly hope—so helpful. Jogging, power-walking, and squats are my go-tos. One of Valentina's classmates told me that he bolts off sprinting when he gets anxious, and it helps him. If a friend of yours is anxious, offering to exercise alongside them might be helpful.

HELP THEM GET GROUNDED.

I just now realized why I like cold Diet Pepsi, hot beverages, Wintergreen Altoids, mint essential oil, yard work, playlists, and stress-eating when I get anxious: all of those things ground me in the present. The basic idea of grounding is to use your five senses to redirect your attention away from the unwanted thoughts or images in your mind by focusing on what is happening in the real-world around you. A common grounding exercise is the 5-4-3-2-1 method:

> **5:** List five things that you see. **4:** List four things that you can feel. **3:** List three things that you hear. **2:** Name two things that you smell. **1:** Name one thing that you taste.

"DO YOU KNOW WHAT YOU'RE ANXIOUS ABOUT?"

If the answer is "no," then ask, "Can you remember what you were doing when you noticed the anxiety starting?" That might help them identify a trigger (or it might not). For Valentina, it was enough to clue her in to her anxiety's root. It usually helps me a lot, too.

If the answer is "yes," then ask them if they want to talk about it. They might not want to. Notice that Valentina didn't. She preferred to process internally. I, too, am an internal processor. Plus, I knew Valentina had plenty of friends she could process with later if she wanted to. It's not about being chosen or rejected as a confidante; it's about supporting people in their moments of need.

"IS THERE ANYTHING I CAN DO TO HELP?"

Answers will vary greatly. You might be asked to give your friend space, to sit together in silence, to listen, to get water, to get someone else, to provide physical touch, to pray, or... well... the list is endless. Just do what you can.

JOHN AND ANNA: KNOWN

Back in 2020, Patrick and I took a rare excursion to a friend's house for pizza and games. We had been getting to know our friends, John and Anna, for the past year through a small group at Restored Church South Bay. John and Anna are almost as weird as we are, so we have good times. That night, when jokes were flying and cards were shuffling, all of a sudden, my anxiety faucet cranked on, hard.

Not now! We need this game night! If I can just fix my anxiety without anyone finding out, maybe the night won't be ruined...

I'm used to things getting ruined when people find out I'm anxious. Things like my remaining shred of sanity, the mood of the room, and the conversation. The spotlight moves away from whatever is going on and lands on me in my fragile, irrational state. Then people throw things at me: platitudes, advice, and pity to name a few. When I'm anxious, I need those things like I need the extra anxiety they cause me.

What I need, actually, is some time alone so I can focus and breathe and do my cognitive journaling. The bathroom is the safest place for that, and I was about to head that way when a surprising thought occurred to me: *I don't have to hide. I can deal with it here,* I thought. *I'm known and safe from the spotlight.*

The small group we all belonged to was full of vulnerable people who gave me the green light to be vulnerable, too. I talked about my anxiety there, on my blog, and on social media. John and Anna are good listeners and readers, and so I knew they understood my relationship with anxiety.

So instead of getting up to go to the bathroom, I did the risky thing and slid my phone out of my pocket, opened my notes app, and tuned out John's lesson on Monopoly Slam so I could journal in my phone. I knew I looked rude, but I didn't care. It was either ignore the humans at the table or risk a potential panic attack, and that would really ruin the evening.

After five minutes of staring at my screen, Patrick asked what I was doing.

"I have some anxiety, and I'm trying to deal with it."

"Oh."

John asked, "Do you know what triggered it?"

"No."

And then Anna said, "You're welcome to use another room, if that would help you."

"Yeah, I think I will, actually. Why don't you guys play the next round and I'll join you when I'm done?"

"Cool, sounds good."

From the couch in the next room, I heard their game start as I closed my eyes and did the things I learned in therapy followed by a bunch of squats. Twenty minutes later, I rejoined them at the table.

Anna casually asked, "How are you feeling?"

"Better. I still have some anxiety, but it usually takes like 30 minutes to work itself out of my system."

"Cool."

"I'll just watch the rest of this round and join in on the next one."

"Sounds good."

And the trash talking and laughing and playing resumed.

At the risk of sounding dramatic, I'm just going to come right out and say it: That night was a breakthrough. I appreciated everyone's casual demeanors. Over the years, I had come to expect people to get hyper-concerned when I confess that I'm anxious. I developed an aversion to the pity-voices people would use. I know those reactions come from a place of care, which I appreciate, but also, it sucks because anxiety attacks are a regular part of my life that I must accept. GAD is a fact of my life, so I appreciate it when others don't treat it as a cataclysmic, piteous tragedy. In rough seasons, for me, it's an everyday occurrence that I manage. I am blessed when my people come alongside me in that.

Chapter 12: Sunday Mornings

When Pastor Calihan's "anxiety and depression are sins" sermon was over, my college-aged peers and I shuffled down our row, joined the current of people exiting the sanctuary, and then gathered outside in the bright June sunshine. I was standing among the socializing crowds when a voice started booming above all the others. It was Tom's. He is a few years older than me, has piercing green eyes, and short brown hair. He was a leader of sorts with an intimidating disposition. In that moment, his voice, like his body and attitude, rose over us. To his assumed audience, he proclaimed,

> I *TOTALLY* get what Pastor Calihan was saying! Church is *exactly* where people need to go when they're struggling with anxiety and depression! Like, I don't get why people stay home from church when they're feeling bad!! It's so *STUPID*! It makes no *SENSE!* When I'm struggling, I know I *NEED* to be at church! It's what makes people *BETTER! UGGGH!*

His lack of empathy and his disdain for the weak in spirit whom Jesus blessed left such an ugly impression on me that it's still here, 20 years later. I take issue with his outburst, but I understand in part where he was coming from. The Apostle Paul *did* say not to give up meeting together, after all.[1] If we only gather with the Church when we feel particularly saintly, charitable, or selfless, then we sort of miss the point of gathering: we gather to be pointed back to Jesus. We gather because we need His grace continuously. We gather to engage with Him. We gather to do all the "one anothers": encourage and love and pray and shepherd and teach and bear with and confess and forgive and give generously. We gather because it's easy to forget the point of life when we are apart from our sisters and brothers. We gather because community is imprinted in our DNA.

Christianity is a communal religion for communities of people designed by a mysteriously communal God who is three in one: Father, Son and Holy Spirit. We are made in the image of that God, which means that we, too, are designed to be in relationship with one another. This is so important to Jesus that just before he was arrested, he prayed that you and I (and even *those Christians*) would live in harmony:

> My prayer is that... all of them may be one, Father, just as you are in me and I am in you... I have given them the glory that you gave me, that they may be one as we are one—I in them and you in me—so that they may be brought to complete unity.[2]

Jesus's prayer wasn't that we would sit next to each other at Sunday services. Church, done right, is not an event or a performance to attend. It isn't a program to participate in or even help lead. Church, done right, is a people—a unified family of sisters and brothers adopted into God's family through the work of God in Jesus Christ. We are called to "lay down [our] lives for one another"[3] and "submit to one another,"[4] as the Apostle Paul instructed the Early Church to do. He told the church in Thessalonica to "encourage the fainthearted, help the weak, be patient with them all,"[5] and he told the church in Galatia to "bear one another's burdens, and so fulfill the Law of Christ."[6] That's a high call. And it's a lot of interaction. I'm afraid that the only interaction many Sunday morning church-goers have is a cheerful greeting and some small talk.

Don't get me wrong. I'm not saying that modern, Western church services are bad (although they certainly *can* be). They are often life-giving, life-changing, and just generally life-y because Jesus said that He is the life, and good church families center around Him. The sharing and teaching of scripture is powerful, as is singing "psalms and hymns and spiritual songs."[7] But spending Sunday mornings in big sanctuaries is not the fully embodied definition of what it means to *be* the Church. This is good news for people like me, because Sunday mornings with an anxiety disorder can be really hard.

SERMONS

Contrary to Tom's assumption that church services cure anxiety attacks, I have often been triggered during church and left in worse shape than when I arrived. Here's how it works.

For starters, most local churches gather in the morning. This is difficult for me because my mind is most fragile in the morning. What doesn't bother me at all midday can send me reeling when I'm just waking up. A therapist once explained that it's because my mind isn't operating at full strength yet, like maybe it needs some time for its defense shields to rise. So when it comes to Sunday morning church gatherings, I do not have the home team advantage.

For this reason, I try my best to avoid anxiety before my church gathers. I want to be wholly receptive during the gathering, so instead of honoring God by showing up early to set up or by volunteering in the kids' classes, when I'm in an anxious season of life, I honor God by embracing my limitations. This means taking it slow and easy: wandering the house in my pjs, enjoying a hot bowl of oatmeal, sitting outside with steaming coffee while watching who's at the birdfeeder. If I need to earn a few endorphins, I take our pup for a brisk walk. Then, when I'm ready, I grab my journal and a cold Spindrift and drive to church with the windows down while listening to my playlist du'jour. I stroll inside, oftentimes late (maybe I should work on that part?), and join my people.

So far, so peaceful. But in anxious seasons, Sunday services can become like minefields: so many opportunities to blow my brain up! Unless you skipped straight to this chapter, you know that a lot of my anxiety gets tangled up in God-related things, and those things happen to take center stage on Sundays. So, minefield.

This is especially true when sermons are *about* anxiety. When Paul's "Be anxious for nothing, but pray about everything," or his "Rejoice in the Lord always!" takes center stage, my brain takes a step forward and CLICK. I freeze and need to *back. up. slowly.*

If I may (and I may—there's no one here to stop me!), a quick side note: I am not against those passages. I am against their overgeneralized misapplication and misinterpretation. To protect against further injuring those of us with thorns stuck in our brains, when preachers at my church, Restored South Bay, reference anxiety or depression, they provide caveats for disorders. They differentiate between "everyone's anxiety" and clinical disorders. In doing so, they acknowledge the grenade my mind just stepped on, and they help me disarm it. They protect me from getting triggered by the false condemnation that I *shouldn't* suffer as I do, that my suffering is all my fault.

Oftentimes, the triggers have nothing to do with anxiety, though. Let's say, for example, that a preacher mentions praying with her spouse. Anxiety might say,

Oh no, oh no, oh no! That doesn't sound like my marriage! Patrick and I don't pray together, hardly ever! Our marriage is doomed and we've been blind this whole time! I'm a failure of a wife and a failure to God!

Sometimes, intrusive thoughts like that get stuck on repeat, but more often than not, they strike like a lightning bolt—visible for a mere millisecond—just long enough to ignite a wildfire of somatic anxiety, but not long enough to leave a thought behind to work through. At that point, my cognitive ability to absorb the rest of the sermon is shot. My brain goes offline. I need to put in the work to get it back online, which means going somewhere I can focus.

So I get up from my seat and head to the bathroom for best odds of successful cognitive journaling. I sit on a toilet rather than a bench outside because some caring person might approach me and ask why I'm alone and if I'm okay. If I say, "Well, I'm anxious right now, and I'm trying to deal with it," I risk eliciting a response that might very well make things worse. And even if no one were to approach me, I'd still be distracted by the possibility that someone *might*. In a way, it's a good thing that I need to hide in bathroom stalls. It's evidence that people care.

Assuming that I am able to journal and breathe my anxiety away, I return to the sanctuary. But that doesn't mean I've made it through all the Sunday landmines yet. At my church, there's still a few worship songs after the sermon.

MUSICAL WORSHIP

Most of the time, worship music helps escort me to the Presence of God alongside my brothers and sisters. But during high-anxiety seasons, it's also fodder for anxiety attacks. If you haven't been triggered by a worship set, that probably sounds pretty backwards, so let me explain. The thoughts, accompanied by their slew of physical symptoms, sometimes go like this:

OMG. These lyrics are so far from my heart. Everyone else here is worshiping so passionately, and my heart feels so cold. If I can't "feel the spirit" now, I never will! I can't even appreciate God's love, and it's infinite! I'm such a failure, such a disappointment!

Before I was diagnosed with GAD, those thoughts were far more frequent because I was regularly and unknowingly going *into* church gatherings in an anxious state. Trying to conjure an emotional experience with God when in a state of fight, flight, or freeze is almost always sure to end poorly. It only exacerbates anxiety. Of course, people don't feel waves of peace and praise when their minds are spiraling uncontrollably. Blaming myself for it only makes it worse.

Nowadays, when anxiety pops up during worship music, I call it out for what it is. I stop singing, sit down, and let the music accompany me as I type in my phone or scribble in my journal. Although I'm no longer meditating on lyrics or singing words, I am still worshiping. Cognitive journaling or using any strategy to become more fully mentally present with God is an act of "loving the Lord your God with all your mind."

A side note. Notice I *sit down* when I get anxious during Sunday church gatherings. It's easier for me to manage anxiety when I'm sitting than it is while standing. Sitting, I can relax all of my muscles. I can focus on breathing more easily. So, if I am anxious when it's time for musical worship to begin, and the leader says, "Stand," I don't. I'm not trying to rebel; I'm just trying to maintain some sanity. I therefore always appreciate it when worship leaders say, "Stand *if you are able*." Those four extra words make me feel seen and included rather than alienated and isolated.

AFTERMATH

A therapist once told me that intense, heightened emotions—even positive ones—can trigger anxiety for those of us with disorders. I've experienced it on plenty of Sundays when the singing or preaching stirs something strong in my spirit. When tears stream down, when lyrics are passionately sung, when things get cathartic, I'm grateful that the Holy Spirit is at work, but sometimes, I also see red flags: my throat cramps, my breathing gets weird, my legs tense and turn hot. When those sensations hit, I know I am in dangerous waters. If I'm not careful, cognitive distortions will easily take over when the music ends. After the last song ends and the benediction is given, when people start chatting and making plans for lunch, my mind is apt to spiral into thoughts like these:

Which group should I go socialize with? No one wants me to join them. I'm just an awkwardly hovering weirdo. I won't belong. I'll just bother them. So I'll stand here by myself. But if I do that, then I'll look uncomfortable, and that will make other people feel uncomfortably sorry for me. Then they'll start freaking out about whether or not to approach me, and then they'll become horribly anxious, and it will all be my fault! I'm making this worse for everyone! AHHH! What should I do with myself?!

And that's my cue to exit. Actually, on Sundays like that, my cue is the benediction. Rather than lingering and socializing and risking decision paralysis, I just make a bee-line for the door. Then at home, I allow my body to process its adrenaline in peace as I dilly dally in my vegetable garden, nap, exercise, snuggle our pup, and commune with Jesus. I can always reach out and catch up with my people later.

LEAVING

In particularly rough anxiety seasons, I drive to church separate from Patrick. That way, I know I'm free to leave without "ruining" (anxiety's wording, not mine) Patrick's plans or my sanity if anxiety becomes unmanageable. And that freedom gives me a little more peace of mind.

Over the seven years I have belonged to Restored, I have left in the middle of gatherings a few times. I do it when my anxiety doesn't respond to bathroom stall journaling sessions or belly breathing or mindfulness or muscle exercises. I leave when I'm desperate to make it stop, but it just won't. I make my exit slyly because the last thing I want on those mornings is a lot of attention.

If I'm going to be anxious, I'd rather be anxious at home. There, I can lay on my bed and dim the lights and sip a cold bubbly drink or a piping hot one and listen to my cathartic playlist and journal and cry hysterically if I need to. The tears don't come from a thing I'm anxious *about;* they come because I'm completely defeated. Recall that Paul used the word "torment" to describe his thorn, and on those days, it's an apt adjective for my lot, too. For me, a good cry on an anxious day is sort of like vomiting on a nauseous day—relief often follows. Naps often follow, too, and I've found that even quick ones reboot my brain.

On those difficult Sundays, both Patrick and I know it's important to handle me with extra care in the afternoon because after a big anxiety attack, it's easy to get re-triggered. So, I spend the rest of the day taking it easy. I don't expect much of myself. I steer clear of things like suspenseful shows, Costco, social media, fast-paced games, and big parties where I only know two people.

STAYING HOME

Every once in a while, I wake up anxious, especially if my hormones have something to do with it. On those days, I stay home from church because there comes a point when showing up for gatherings becomes foolish. Having a chronic illness, whether physical or mental, requires the ill among us to exercise our discernment. We have good days and bad days, good weeks and bad weeks, good months and bad months. Heck, I've had good *years* of remission and hard years of reignition.

In general, it is unwise and often impossible to show up for events—sacred or secular—while writhing in pain, panicked beyond functionality, or sedated by necessary medication. Recently, I had one of those mornings. Although I craved fellowship, I stayed home so I could treat, rather than exacerbate, my symptoms. While my church family was meeting, I was sitting on my couch, where I scribbled something in my journal that became this poem:

JESUS WAS LONELY, TOO

When things get hard,
And anxiety leaves you isolated
(because you must heal)
And when your calling
leads you to solitude
(like, say, to write)
And when your career leaves you
Just minutes with colleagues
(because you teach)
And your personality type
Is called rare
(like INFP)[8]
And when your pain disorder
Leaves you home with ice and heat

And you're tired—

Remember—
Jesus
the Suffering Servant
understands.
He knew loneliness
far deeper.
And so it's okay for
me to feel this way, too.
He is in it
with me,
Never leaving me
alone. <3

As I put down my pen, I got some notifications from a thread Patrick and I have with our friend, Luma. The two of them were texting about how good the sermon was. There were crying emojis and everything. Our friend, Erick, had preached it. I, of course, had missed it. But the Spirit encouraged me to do what

I could, so I took a screenshot of their words and forwarded it to Erick along with these words:

> Hey bro. The Spirit moved through you today. :) I'm gonna listen during my commute this week. Woke up with rough anxiety and some jaw pain so decided to hibernate in hopes of healing!

A few minutes later, I got a response:

> Aww I'm really encouraged to hear that the Spirit moved. Thank you for sharing. Also, I'm bummed you're going through that, sis. Glad you took some much needed time to rest. Let us know if we can help in some way, like dropping some foods off or anything that comes to mind.

I looked up from my phone with teary eyes because unlike Tom, Pastor Callihan, and so many others from my past, Erick believed me and supported me in my struggle. He did not chastise me for missing his sermon or not having "enough faith" to show up despite what my body needed. He didn't blame my anxiety on my spirituality. His response is a true manifestation of what it looks like to "encourage the fainthearted and help the weak."

Being part of this beautiful church family makes me *want* to serve on Sundays alongside my sisters and brothers, but during high-anxiety seasons, when I can barely show up on Sundays, it's not realistic to sign up for extra responsibilities.

Chapter 13: Serving

Patrick joined the "Hospitality Team" at Restored soon after we started attending, which meant that on Sundays, he often showed up a couple hours early to set things up and stayed an hour later to break things down. It felt expected that I should help, too. (It wasn't, but I felt like it was.) Unlike all the young parents at our church, we didn't have any kids to get ready and rush out the door. If Patrick could help, why couldn't I? I didn't have an excuse for sleeping in, or at least none that my new church family could see. Invisible illness is sneaky and humbling like that.

Patrick soon dove into other opportunities to help the church with technical and physical needs. He served so much and I so little that I suspected others of viewing me as Patrick's spiritually immature wife, some luke-warm sloth who was unwilling to invest any time or sweat in eternity.

While my assumption was entirely unfounded, it was true that my position wasn't impressive, namely because I had none. I wasn't serving in family ministry or the youth group or the hospitality team, or anything. It wasn't because I didn't want to. I did want to, mostly because at that time, I was new at church, temporary at work, and no longer sure of my purpose in life. Of course, I wanted to contribute. Of course, I wanted to be part of something bigger than myself. Of course, I wanted to be known. I wanted the leaders to know that I was like them, that I too had experiences and strengths and wisdom—or something—to offer. And how would they know unless I showed them?

At that time though, there wasn't much I could do, especially on Sundays. I was in the midst of the season that Dr. Carraway warned me about a decade earlier: the one involving a life transition major enough to trigger a resurgence of my GAD. I was on that six-month waitlist to see a psychiatrist so I could change my meds. My professional life was being strangled by a broken system, my calling to write this book was solitary and confusing, and more days than not, my energy and concentration were drained by intractable anxiety. I didn't have much to offer.

It was natural and human of me to long to belong, but the compulsion to prove myself to others was not healthy. Jesus never called anyone to impress their leaders or distribute polished spiritual resumes. He himself was grossly misunderstood, especially by the religious leadership of his day, so why should I, as his disciple, expect otherwise?

Seeking a sense of purpose from an official position on a ministry team wasn't the best. It wasn't the Holy Spirit inspiring me to serve; it was a deceitful chorus of insecurity, loneliness, and purposelessness. My flesh's default mode is to calculate my value according to my perceived impact on the world around me. In that anxious season, the math got pretty ugly, because anxiety and loneliness rendered me pretty helpless.

Like me and my "impact," the religious leaders of Jesus's day, the Pharisees, derived their identity and worth from their religious positions rather than from the God they claimed to represent. Jesus called them out and instructed all of us to be different: "Be careful not to practice your righteousness in front of others to be seen by them. Otherwise, you have no reward with your Father in heaven."[1]

I confess that I like honor and respect and status. I want others to think I am valuable. It helps *me* feel valuable (for a time). However, it doesn't *make* me valuable.

God's math is simple, but it doesn't come easy: our true value is derived solely from His value of us, and thank God, that never changes. Resting in that Truth is where the deepest joy is found. I am of use and worth and value and importance regardless of where I happen to fall on anxiety's spectrum of debilitation on any given day or week or month or year. My value is independent of others' understanding of why I serve or don't serve. God knows my capacity. He *gives* me that capacity. May I be faithful with it.

Cognitively, I'd known that Truth for decades. But I didn't know it in my bones. I didn't know it experientially. Through temporarily removing my ability to serve in obvious, visible capacities, God gifted me with the deeper-rooted Truth that my identity and value exist independently of any impact I do or do not make.

COPPER COINS AND CAPACITY

One day, Jesus was chilling with his disciples, watching people coming and going from the synagogue as they made donations. Jesus's friend, Mark, recalled what he saw.

> Many rich people put in large sums. And a poor widow came and put in two small copper coins, which make a penny. And [Jesus] called his disciples to him and said to them, 'Truly, I say to you, this poor widow has put in more than all those who are contributing to the offering box. For they all contributed out of their abundance, but she out of her poverty has put in everything she had, all she had to live on.'[2]

Jesus knew that woman's limited resources, and he knows the resources each of us is working with: financial, mental, physical, and otherwise. He knows signing up to serve is an act of faith when anxiety attacks make capacity unpredictable. He understands that showing up is an act of courage. He knows we might have to leave early. He knows when others "contribute out of their abundance" of mental and emotional wealth, and when you "out of your poverty put in everything you have." In the eyes that matter, your pennies of mental and emotional energy are worth just as much—if not more—than the thousands donated by those who have been given abundant stores of the stuff.

Living with fluctuating capacity is tricky. It seems like just when I get used to living with five pennies, the season changes and I come into fifty thousand dollars of the stuff. It's hard to know when and to what extent to adjust my expectations of myself and my capacity to serve.

This is okay. Scripture teaches that "there is a time for everything, and a season for every activity under the heavens:

>   a time to be born and a time to die,
>   a time to plant and a time to uproot,
>   a time to kill and a time to heal,
>   a time to tear down and a time to build,
>   a time to weep and a time to laugh,
>   a time to mourn and a time to dance,
>   a time to scatter stones and a time to gather them,
>   a time to embrace and a time to refrain from embracing,
>   a time to search and a time to give up,
>   a time to keep and a time to throw away,
>   a time to tear and a time to mend,
>   a time to be silent and a time to speak,
>   a time to love and a time to hate,
>   a time for war and a time for peace."[3]

Everyone's seasons change, but it seems that mental illness makes the weather within life's seasons more fickle and intense. It causes more hurricanes, flash floods, and earthquakes. When those disasters strike, they force survivors to reprioritize and reorganize their lives until the wreckage is cleared and wounds are healed. That might look like stepping down from a volunteer role for a while. It might look like taking a couple sick days. It might look like leaving in the middle of your small group.

It might look like canceling even though you RSVP'd "yes." It might look like flaking. But really, you're not. You were hit by a monsoon. You would much rather be at the party, but your house must be rebuilt. And that's okay, because "there is a time for everything, and a season for every activity under the heavens."

There is a time to sign up and a time to step down,
a time to call a sub and a time to show up, however hesitant,
a time to say "yes" and a time to say "no,"
a time to do the thing despite the anxiety and a time
to just not,
a time to avoid triggers and a time to face them,
a time to show up in courage and a time to hang back in wisdom,
a time to hold fast and survive and a time to lean back and enjoy,
a time to seek support and a time to give it.

One of the trickiest things about natural disasters is that they're hard to predict. It's easier to ride out storms when you can see them coming, however last-minute the warning. While I can't know for sure when I'm heading into a stormy season, over the years, I have learned some things about my weather patterns.

My dark clouds look like a lot of people's. For one, significant life transitions tend to foreshadow seasons of struggle. I told you about how our big relocation from Northern California to San Diego reawakened my GAD. In the years that followed, I learned to anticipate chronic anxiety storms whenever it was time to start teaching at a new school. I've also noticed that anxiety is more likely to loom during PMS and on Sundays.

Everyone's storm clouds look different. The important thing is to study your life and look for weather patterns. A therapist or wise friend can be quite helpful. Then, when you spot purple clouds hovering over the horizon, you can hunker down a bit. When I see my ominous clouds, I practice self-care more diligently. I get more selective when it comes to my commitments.

I ask my friends for prayer. I protect my Sabbath rest more fiercely.

If a storm lasts for days and weeks and months, and if months stretch into stormy years, hold on. It won't be in vain. Storms do pass. When I hunkered down for those first six months in San Diego, life didn't feel very fruitful. But the weather eventually cleared up, and in hindsight, I now see that God was doing the greater work of shaping my heart into its Truer form. He was pulling apart my worth from my works while gifting me with this story to share. Weathering that storm was painful and stretching, but in retrospect, I am somehow better for it. I am more wholly me, more wholly His, and more grateful for sunny seasons.

NOT DISQUALIFIED

While mental illness brings with it seasons that might require stepping back from commitments and ministries, it by no means disqualifies us from the good work God has prepared in advance for each of us to do.[4] Jesus doesn't set us up for failure. The fact that 25% of pastors report struggling with mental illness is proof.[5] They are *still* pastoring. Jesus guides and carries them through their struggles as they care for the flocks He entrusts to them. I've had a successful 16-year teaching career despite all the craziness this book speaks to. Perseverance *is* a thing. Navigating it all sure isn't easy, though. That's why we must depend on Jesus to guide and sustain us, and then rest in the fact that He takes care of all that we can't.

In sunnier seasons, I often serve in more committed capacities. Sometimes on Sundays, I deliver announcements from the stage. I've been serving as a Young Life committee member for seven years. Back in my twenties and into my thirties, I did direct ministry with teenagers as a volunteer Young Life leader. I've also co-led small groups during the week, and I imagine I will again.

The "co" in "co-led" matters. Knowing that responsibility does not solely fall on my shoulders helps keep anxiety at bay. I can rely on a ministry partner to help carry the load if anxiety shows up. Plus, you know, Jesus sent people out in pairs, so there's probably something to it.[6] As we consider what it looks like to serve inside and outside of our local churches throughout our various seasons, it is important to strive for self-awareness, discernment, and honesty with ourselves and our people, especially with the leaders who oversee the ministries in which we serve. I want leaders to know that I'm capable, but sometimes short on capacity. I want them to know my strengths and give me opportunities to contribute, but I also want to give them opportunities to support me and help me thrive. If I don't tell them about what's going on with me, how can they do that?

Take, for example, this crazy thing I did a few months back. I signed up to do the thing I intentionally didn't do when we first joined Restored: I joined the team that helps set up and tear down the sanctuary on Sundays. My season had gone from typhoons to clear-ish skies, my church needed the help, and I wanted to give back. *It might work,* I hoped. Plus, the commitment was only once a month. The team is led by Priscilla, a pretty brunette with two little boys. She helped plant our church and serves as a deacon. Before I reached out to her, I let the idea mull in the back of my mind for a few weeks. *Was* this a good idea? There was only one way to find out. I texted Priscilla:

> Hey Pris, I've been contemplating joining the hospitality team for a little while now, and thought I'd make a move on it. So yah, I'm down! The only caveat is if my anxiety disorder flares up for a season, I'll have to step down.

Priscilla responded:

> I would LOVE to have you join the hospitality team! I'm SO encouraged by your obedience in not wanting to live in the 'what ifs.' I know God will meet you in it! I will add you to

the Planning Center, and if you have moments where the anxiety flares up, you can always tell me. I can always find a sub or jump in myself!

I know not all ministry leaders are as understanding as Priscilla is. I know the presence of stigma in any community makes vulnerability exponentially scarier. I know not all pastors got their bachelor's in psychology like my pastor Danny did. So, take that last part with a grain of salt. But a lot has improved in the world of faith and mental health over these last couple decades. You might be pleasantly surprised if and when you dip your toe in the pool of vulnerability and divulge your struggle with a fellow believer. I recommend starting with people who feel safest. If you try being honest with a leader and it doesn't go well, then send them this book and drop the mic. (It feels pompous to equate my own book with a mic drop, but to be honest, it was part of the dream when I started this project.)

These days, I'm learning to work with the capacity I'm given when I have it, whether it's a fortune or a penny. Maybe this is the kind of thing the Apostle Paul was talking about when he said, "I have learned to live in plenty and in want."[7] When I've been living in want for a while, though, hunkering down to tend to my hurting brain, I start feeling down. I start to feel like I don't belong because I have to withdraw. I start to feel like I'm just suffering from the sidelines while everyone else is in the game. When ministry teams and small group leaders are at appreciation dinners and trainings and team building activities, it's easy to feel left out and wonder where I belong.

Chapter 14: Belonging and the Body

Patrick and I vividly recall our second Sunday at Restored. We sat in folding chairs in the back of a school's multipurpose room in complete shock. We couldn't believe what we were hearing from the stage. A married couple stood there. They were choking on their words, because infidelity is hard to swallow, let alone share with 150 people, including one of their parents. Their story is messy: a few years prior, one of them cheated, and the emotions understandably oozed as they picked at the scab in front of everyone. They welcomed us into the dark, sacred place where sin and pain nearly broke them. They testified to the ongoing redemptive work Jesus was doing in their lives as a result of it.

I soon found that the same questions they answered from the stage were a staple among my new church community: "What are you becoming? How is God changing and shaping you? How is Jesus saving you? How are you living?"

Answering those questions requires an admission of present weakness and sinfulness, which most people commit to denial or distraction. They certainly don't broadcast them into microphones; that is, not unless their leaders do it first. Thank Jesus, our leaders at Restored South Bay do. Sermons in our church community are always served with a healthy dose of vulnerability:

"I need to be honest with you guys... I struggled so much to write this sermon because I'm not very good at living it out."

"I'm feeling really nervous about this message today... Do you guys mind if we just stop and pray for a minute?"

"Last month my therapist pointed out that..."

"Last week, my wife and I were arguing, and I said something so messed up that we were both shocked."

"I'm seeing my kids adopting my own sinful behavior..."

Thirty-some years in churches, and I'd never heard pastors and preachers confess their current, specific sins and struggles like these ones do. Sure, I'd heard a pastor confess to speeding on the freeway. I'd heard leaders vaguely allude to Paul's words: "For I do not do the good I want to do, but the evil I do not want to do—this I keep on doing."[1] And one time, in front of his congregation, a pastor confessed to yelling at a skateboarder (who recognized him) in a parking lot a few days earlier.

All of this is to say that I spent my entire life immersed in the cultural expectation that church leaders should live holier lives, be more spiritually mature, and have a sturdier faith than the people in their congregations. There is Truth in that, but taken too far, it becomes problematic.

In any given church, the pastor will not always be the strongest, holiest person, nor should they be. We all have seasons of nearness and distance from our Savior, seasons of rejoicing and despairing, church staff not excluded. Pastors are as fallible and fragile as the rest of us. They are trying to keep pace after the same infallible Jesus we are, and in that regard, we are all equals before Him.

When pastors reveal how Jesus specifically meets them in their faults and failures, they help us see Jesus at work in our own lives, too. That lays a foundation of the Gospel, the central story of Everything. True Christianity, unlike other religions, has never been about performance, perfection, or good-enoughs; therefore, that is not what we need to see from church leaders. Gospel-centered pastors and sermons do not simply teach us to do better, try harder, know more, or be more obedient. Those messages alone tend to be more like the gospel of the Pharisees whom Jesus regularly rebuked. What we need are leaders who let us in on their messy, some-steps-forward, some-steps-backward, flesh-versus-spirit walk with Jesus.

I need to see what it honestly looks like to follow Jesus down today's dusty paths:

What does it look like to get tired, to lose heart, and drag your feet?

What does it look like when you forget to look up and then find yourself lost and alone?

What does it look like to get distracted and stumble and bleed?

What does it look like to be found over and over and over again?

And what does it look like to grasp the hand He offers, and trust Him to pull you back up?

What does it look like to get caught up in zeal and jog right past Him?

How do you make things right with all the people who are choking on all the dust you kicked up along the way?

And what does it look like to follow while you wait?

What the Church needs most from her leaders is for them to reveal the Gospel at work in their lives, so that the rest of us can see it in ours, too. Leaders point us to the Most Important Thing when they confess their own ways of "falling short of the Glory of God," their inability to fix themselves, their dependence on Jesus to redeem and restore them, and Jesus's faithfulness in doing just that.

I used to think of the Gospel as the entry point to Christianity, a door through which we enter and then progress beyond. But my new church family has been helping me see that the Gospel is not merely a step in our spiritual journey, but it is the place where we live it out. Its depths are infinite. Our need for our Savior is constant. His redemption of our weakness and sin is ongoing. It's a profound and beautiful reality.

Unfortunately, in this world of distractions and demands, it is easy to forget. To help us remember, we practice spiritual disciplines. We study and meditate on scripture, we commune with our Creator in prayer, we take communion as Jesus taught, we sing the Truth, we remind one another of the Truth. And because He loves us, his Holy Spirit "guides us into all Truth."[2]

When we pay attention to our lives, we can see the Gospel there, too. Vulnerable leaders are helping me to notice it more often. For example, I've had some sort of savior complex as far back as I can remember, but I was blind to it until my pastor Danny preached a sermon in which he shared personal stories that illustrate his own struggle with playing the role of savior. He explained his failure to honor his limitations and rest in God's sovereignty. I recognized the parallels in my own life and was therefore able to surrender my need to be needed to the One True Savior.

Pastors like Danny help me become more self-aware, which isn't always comfortable, but is always healthy. When he shares his own weakness and sin, doors to the Gospel swing open, because if my pastor still needs Jesus to save him, then I must, too. And the good news is that Jesus always extends grace to us. When this Truth is experienced as a congregation, we grow in unity and love for one another, too.

In church communities like Restored, ones that practice vulnerability from the top-down, there is room for me and my tribe to belong. Those of us with thorns in our flesh are well aware of our weakness. The throbbing can't be ignored. It helps us remain self-aware of how desperately we need Jesus. Our thorns protect us from the deception that we don't need God. We therefore thrive in church communities that strive to abide in that same Truth.

It comes as no surprise then, that we struggle to belong in church communities that value impact and success above need and grace. Believers like me who struggle with mental health become emotional outsiders at churches that celebrate power and prosperity more than humility and righteousness. Preachers at those churches avoid sharing their weaknesses—both the kinds that are their fault and the kinds that aren't—and their congregations follow suit. People only let their strengths show. Those of us who are stabbed by thorns start to feel alone and ashamed. We start to see our weakness as weakness, rather than strength, as Paul and Jesus proclaimed. We hide our struggles and put on masks of self-reliance to fit in. Then, when it all becomes too exhausting, we either leave or break through the ceiling of strength with raw honesty.

When leaders do not demonstrate their need for God, they miss opportunities to share the Gospel with believers and non-believers alike. The people they shepherd become less likely to see God at work in their own lives. They are more likely to get caught up in lesser things and develop identities outside of Christ.

Unfortunately, I'm not aware of too many churches that celebrate weakness. I'm not saying that all churches should be like mine. I'm not some zealous patriot of Restored South Bay. Like all organizations comprised of humans, we have our issues. But the celebration of weakness is something that I hope I get to see more churches develop. The Apostle Paul did it. He found such profound purpose in his weakness that instead of bragging about his ministry, his influence, his brand, or his following, he bragged about his weakness.

> Most gladly... I will boast about my weaknesses, so that the power of Christ may dwell in me... I am well content

with weaknesses, with insults, with distresses, with persecutions, with difficulties, for Christ's sake; for when I am weak, then I am strong.³

While it is counterintuitive to showcase the shattered parts of ourselves, when we do, we also get to explain how God meets us in our need, how He heals us, and how He redeems us. The more in tune we are with our own humanness, the more able we are to connect with fellow humans and point them toward Jesus.

BELONGING WHEN IT'S HARD

Even in church families that practice vulnerability and honor weakness, mental illness can make belonging difficult. This is partially because by its nature, mental illness is isolating. It separates me from my brain. From my *self*. It should come as no surprise, then, that it separates me from other people, too. A significant aspect of belonging is showing up, contributing, and being on mission together. Flare-ups and episodes of all sorts can cripple us and send us to the sidelines.

When anxiety puts me out of commission for a season, and I find myself having to say "no" to a lot of events and opportunities, it is important to feel my feelings and grieve the fact that I'm missing out. And then after a little while, it's important to recall the words of Dr. Martin Luther King, Jr.:

> If you can't fly, then run. If you can't run, then walk. If you can't walk, then crawl, but whatever you do, you have to keep moving forward.

Those words remind me to think about the things I *can* do to belong and contribute. Many of them are things that give me joy and flexibility so that I can engage in them when my mental health allows.

For example, in a difficult season, I *can* encourage a preacher by sharing a text. I *can* pray and intercede for others (how huge and accessible that ministry is!). I can offer my backyard for Young Life events. I can share my obnoxiously oversized garden zucchinis. I can write. I can stay at the ER with a new friend until 2am. I can make Easter baskets for teen parents and their littles. I can babysit my friends' kids for a couple hours so they can go to couples therapy. I can attend Young Life Committee meetings on Saturday mornings. I can check in with people over text or food or drinks. I can fellowship with my "Mentally Unstable Stable Club." I can send a random card to my sister or my bestie. I can help people on the periphery feel welcome. All of these things are "being the body" just as much as serving on a rostered, visible "serve team" that I can't consistently show up for during stormy seasons.

While it's important for me to "keep moving forward," it's also not entirely on me to nurture my own sense of belonging. I do what I can, but I also need to rest in the fact that the body of Christ is called to be *interdependent*. The scriptures liken the relationships of Christ followers to the relationships of different parts of one body. Paul discusses this interdependence in a letter to the church in Corinth:

> The eye cannot say to the hand, "I don't need you!" And the head cannot say to the feet, "I don't need you!" On the contrary, those parts of the body that seem to be weaker are indispensable, and the parts that we think are less honorable we treat with special honor. And the parts that are unpresentable are treated with special modesty, while our presentable parts need no special treatment. But God has division in the body, but that its parts should have equal concern for each other. If one part suffers, every part suffers with it; if one part is honored, every part rejoices with it.[4]

I am one of "those parts of the body that seem to be weaker," but am in fact "indispensable." (Did you notice that? We weak ones are *indispensable!*) As members of the body of Christ, seasons of suffering should never be seasons of isolation. When my foot is suffering, I know it. It's on my mind, and I tend to it. If we are really a body, the other parts will feel my suffering, too. Like nerves delivering messages from pain receptors, it is healthy for me to communicate my pain to the body to which I belong, and it is healthy for them to tend to that pain.

Last year, I started sending SOS texts to my small group from church when anxiety attacked at work. My friends prayed in real time, and I swear, every time, either my anxiety abated or my class calmed. It reminds me of Jesus calming the storm. Through His Spirit, shared by His body—the Church—He is still calming storms.[5]

My friends from small group help me endure and heal, and I try to do likewise when their parts ache. In the process, we become a healthier, more effective whole while offering one another opportunities to fulfill Jesus's command to love one another sacrificially. They listen and are slow to speak. They pray. They ask questions. They encourage.

However, there is one thing (okay, probably a lot of things) most of my friends can't do: they can't commiserate. They don't share my brand of suffering. And don't get me wrong—they have awful things in their stories that I can't (thankfully) commiserate with (yet). They have buried moms and dads and siblings and children and lost unborn babies. They have survived sexual abuse, child abuse and neglect, gang violence, unfaithful spouses, poverty, liver failure (and thankfully, successful transplants)—awful things. While we experience profound fellowship together, there is simply something extra offered when people get the blessed opportunity to fellowship with others who share their same brand of suffering.

TRIBE

One evening in 2019, I was relaxing on the couch when my phone rang. The name on my caller ID was intriguing: "Danny Restored." We'd talked on occasion, but a phone call was a first. After exchanging pleasantries, he explained his reason for calling: "I'm doing a sermon on Paul's thorn on Sunday, and I would really love to quote some of your writing that you shared online. Would that be ok?"

Heaven opened, and the angels sang! Okay, maybe they didn't, but it was a beautiful moment. Of course, I said yes. I also agreed to be available to pray for people after the sermon.

When Sunday rolled around, mid-sermon, a paragraph of mine appeared on the huge projector screen. Danny read it with *umph*, and when he was done, people clapped. Some even stood. And then as he wrapped up his sermon and the band approached the stage, he extended an invitation: "If you're struggling with mental health, Tiffany will be available in the back for prayer."

During the closing songs, people rose from their seats one at a time and walked toward me until there were 15 or 20 of us standing together. I gestured to huddle up. Then I stepped into the middle, took a deep breath, and the Spirit helped me pray some prayer like this:

"Jesus, thank you for these sisters and brothers. Thank you for giving them boldness to get up from their chairs and gather here. Jesus, You know each of us intimately, and You know exactly what our struggles are. You know how hard it is. And you know firsthand what it feels like. You are God who sweat blood in Gethsemane.

Father, please remind us of your presence when we feel alone in it. Encourage us. Give us glimpses of how you're redeeming our pain. May we know that it's not for nothing, but that You restore all things painful and broken. Jesus, You know how hard it can be. You experienced greater anxiety than we ever will. You felt a heavier burden than we ever will. Thank you that you are near, even when it doesn't feel that way.

Lord, I pray for these sisters and brothers, that You would equip them with endurance and perseverance and encouragement and support. I pray for healing, that you would give them relief from their symptoms. Jesus, You love each of us so, so much. Help keep the lies at bay. Help us to see You. Thank You that we are never alone. Amen."

We opened our eyes and looked at one other. Some faces sparkled with tears. I knew maybe half of them. Some of us hugged, some lingered and chatted, and a couple weeks later, some of us started meeting up at a local coffee shop. Mostly, we listened and commiserated and comforted and encouraged one another. I didn't know what I was doing, except for showing up for my people.

Our group morphed over the years. People moved. Some just moved on. But they will always be my tribe. And today I have Vanessa and Jordan and Elizabeth and Anne and other people from church who know what it's like. We meet up at beaches and Novo Hard Kombucha. Those places become churches when we are there. We share raw, sacred moments as we invite one another into our stories and struggles. We share battle stories from OCD, GAD, BPD, ADHD, and depression. We lament the pain that our thorns inflict on our friendships and relationships. We say things like, "So, basically, I'm a full-blown alcoholic now, guys," and "I used sex just to feel something," and "I just can't bring myself to walk through church doors yet," and "Did I just ruin my relationship?" and "Why is it so hard for me to just call a therapist?" We use hard language to convey the hard realities our minds spin out behind our eyes. We rant. And cry. And counsel. And point each other back to Jesus and back to Hope, over and over and over again. And we laugh. A lot.

Our presence in each other's lives reinforces God's Truth that we're never alone. Our fellowship is marked by the vulnerability of our church family and the brand of suffering that must be experienced to be fully appreciated. With them, I feel understood and known. Like this one Sunday. The sermon had just started, and I was sitting alone in a middle row. I was feeling like the only one who had spent the last week with a crazy brain. I was tired. Disconnected. Uninvolved. Not understood. Not understandable. And then my friend Jordan showed up, 20 minutes late. She's a young mom, cute and tiny, with dark, curly hair. I know her relentless OCD, her trauma, her church hurt. I know her struggle to muster the motivation to find a new therapist. I know how sometimes she feels like she's going crazy in the same way that I do. And she has three tiny boys on top of it all. I don't know how she does it, except "with God, all things are possible." The sermon had already begun. She shimmied down my row and landed next to me. We exchanged a whispered "hi." And instantly, I belonged.

Appendix

THANK YOU...

To my parents for raising me with Love and confidence to do things like this.

To Patrick for supporting me through this crazy calling and putting up with all the times I've been "almost done."

To Justin McRoberts, whose music shaped my faith and whose guidance shaped this book.

To Reese Roper and Five Iron Frenzy: Your authenticity, humility, and art have been like a trellis for my soul. You're the worst.

To my brilliant friends who became volunteer editors: LaNeida, Nancy, and Anna (who also became my brilliant book designer!).

To all my friends and family who let me hide their stories in these pages.

To my Kickstarter supporters for your faith in me and this project.

To anyone who ever "liked" or commented on my posts: Your encouragement kept me going.

To whoever sent me *The Coloring Book for Writers* during the pandemic and said it was from Jesus. (*Was it??*)

To Danny and my Restored South Bay family: For modeling how vulnerability brings us back to Jesus.

To the Mentally Unstable Stable Club: for the laughter, tears, and rants that remind me I'm not alone.

To Young Life South Bay: for all the beautiful miracles you invite me into.

To my local school districts for the crappy contracts and unstable employment. How could I have finished this while teaching full time?

Acey and Maddy: Woof!

Most of all— to that Still, Small Voice who whispered, "Not yet," when I wanted to write something meaningful at 21. Without You, I'd have no story.

Questions for Discussion or Reflection

I tried not to create this section.

It's funny how you can read something 317 times and not be struck by it until the 318th. That's what happened to me while editing chapter three for the 318th time: One of my own sentences suddenly compelled me to create this section. The culpable passage comes from the part about the book club I was in with Kim, Bridget, and Jess. (If you haven't reached that part yet, sorry for the spoiler, but there's a book club in this book. It's a literary nesting doll!)

Anyway, it goes like this:

> My new friends voiced opinions that often go unspoken at church groups: we disagreed with the author, laughed at his cheesy anecdotes, and made fun of the book's ridiculously long title. For all its quirks though, God certainly worked through that book. It was about trusting Jesus and taking chances, and *it came with discussion questions, which prompted us to talk about real things.*

If the whole point of *Anxious with Jesus* is to foster some fellowship at the intersection of faith and mental illness, why not add discussion questions? Apparently, I had my reasons. Or... well... excuses:

1. I had already spent seven years on this book project. At some point, I just had to be *done*. And I wanted to be done *now*.
2. Books don't *need* discussion questions. The feature smelled like extra-credit. As a (hopefully?) recovering perfectionist, I've learned to suspect the stench of above-and-beyond. Sort of.
3. Laziness. I've been unemployed for nine months now. Add that to my Type B personality, and apparently it's easy for me to acclimate to the assumption that I don't *need* to do much. Extra book sections included.

But then factors beyond my control pushed my publication timeline back, and writing discussion questions practically became a *why-not* situation. Still, I dragged my feet. I suspect God wanted this section to happen, though, because a friend from church asked me if I wanted to lead a discussion group for my book when it comes out. A week later, another friend from Young Life asked me to lead the same kind of group for young adults. The evidence and arguments mounted against my laziness and convinced me to push this section out.

So, here it is. If you benefit from these questions in any way, please thank Jesus, because if it were simply up to me, some mash-up of tiredness and laziness would have convinced me not to bother. He really is pursuing you in love. <3

So, without further adieu, here's my best shot at stimulating conversation and friendship among you, my beloved readers.

SOME TIPS FOR DISCUSSION

The way I see it, there are a couple ways to discuss this book. First is the organic route. Simply read with a pen or highlighter within arm's reach and mark the parts that strike you. Feel free to explore and reflect on those parts individually through journaling. Then when your group meets, respond to the question,

"What stood out to you from the reading?" Take turns sharing what you highlighted and why. As people share, you can ask follow-up questions, share about similar experiences, encourage, and pray for one another.

I know doing those things can be scary. For those of my brothers and sisters who have Social Anxiety Disorder, I know it can be exponentially harder. You don't have to share everything. What you process as you read (and journal) is between you and God. At first, allow yourself to just show up to your discussion group and listen. As you get a little more comfortable, consider pre-selecting just one thing to share. You can read straight from your journal if you like. Ease in. Give the Spirit space to work.

If you're not sure where to start—whether with journaling or sharing—here are some sentence frames that might help:

I felt seen when... because...

This part helped me better understand...

Before reading, I thought/felt .... But now I think/feel...

I wonder...

Reading this made me feel...

This reminds me of...

This inspires/challenges me to...

... resonates with me...

I want to try...

I don't understand/agree with...

The second approach for discussing this book is to use the chapter-specific questions included in the following pages. A leader or facilitator can pre-select which ones to discuss, or alternatively, group members can refer to any question and then respond to it ("I'd like to answer number ___ ..."). The downside of relying entirely on the chapter questions is that it limits conversation: a group member might long to talk about something not covered in them. My personal preference is a combination of both: Open with "What stood out to you?" and then use chapter-specific questions to encourage further conversation. Do whatever works best for your group!

STRUCTURED QUESTION FORMAT

INTRODUCTION:

1. What are your first impressions of this book? What do you hope to take from it?
2. What are your hopes and fears about participating in this group?
3. Can you relate to Tiffany's longing to find someone who could relate to her? How so?
4. You already know how the story ends: God uses Tiffany to write and publish the book she wanted to read. What does this suggest about the nature of God? What does it suggest about your own story?

1: EARLY YEARS

1. What was your upbringing like? Do any aspects of Tiffany's childhood or adolescence resonate with yours?
2. Did religion play a role in your upbringing? In what way(s) was it a positive or negative experience?
3. Share about a time when a small gesture, conversation, or act of kindness made a big impact on you (like when the upperclassmen remembered Tiffany's name).
4. Tiffany suffered from manifestations of anxiety long before she was able to identify it as such. Can you relate to this? Explain.

5. Recall that "bands like Five Iron Frenzy and the Supertones became deeply influential in the formation of [Tiffany's] identity and faith." Other than your family of origin, who or what have been influential in the formation of your identity and/or faith? Consider artists, bands, writers, pastors, mentors, videos, podcasts, etc.

`2: ONSET: WHEN I DIDN'T FEEL LIKE ME

1. Have you ever experienced a shift in your mental health that was confusing, disorienting, and/or hard to explain? Have you ever confused symptoms of mental illness for sin? At what point did you receive clarity (if you did)?

2. Does your mental health (or neurodivergence) ever affect your ability to pray, read scripture, engage in musical worship, or participate in fellowship?

3. Can you recall a sermon that left a lasting impression on you (for better or for worse)?

4. Do you struggle with thoughts or beliefs (about God) that feel real, even though you know deep down they are false? If so, what is the lie, and what is the Truth? Do you have any tips or strategies that have helped you in this area?

3: ON SINKING AND SAVING

1. Tiffany shared how *Scrubs* spoke to her during her loneliest season of life. Is there a show, movie, song, or other form of art that brings you comfort and company when things get hard?

2. Who has helped you during your lows in life? What did they do that was helpful?

3. Have you walked alongside someone else through a difficult season in their life? What did that look like?

4. Have you ever suggested to someone that they seek professional help? Has someone suggested it to you? How did it go?

5. Tiffany's anxiety affected her ability to be an effective teacher. How have mental health issues affected areas of your life (relationships, career, family, school, ministry etc.)? To what extent have you experienced healing, and to what extent is the struggle ongoing?

6. Tiffany wrote, "It is that heart of flesh that allows His followers to selflessly seek out people whose needs, by the grace of God, we just might be able to meet." How open are your eyes to the people on your periphery "whose needs, by the grace of God, you might just be able to meet"? Are there people you could invite into your life like Kim, Jess, and Bridget invited Tiffany in?

Challenge: Submit your comfort to Jesus and ask Him to give you eyes to see the people around you as He does. Ask for faithfulness to act on whatever He might reveal to you.

7. To what extent is it difficult for you to "let people in"? Why do you think that is?

Challenge: Consider what it would look like to be more vulnerable with one or more people in your life and ask Jesus for courage and wisdom as you allow yourself to become more known.

8. Have you experienced "church hurt"? Have you healed from it? What did that look like?

4: DIAGNOSIS

1. Share about your own mental health journey: What do you struggle with? Have you been diagnosed with a disorder? If so, what did you think and feel when you received that diagnosis? In what way(s) was the diagnosis helpful (or unhelpful)?

2. Do you suspect you might have a disorder? Are you open to looking into it? Why or why not?

3. To what extent was Tiffany's analogy about TB and the radio a helpful illustration of everyone's anxiety and anxiety disorders? Did it help you make sense of it?

4. Have you experienced physical symptoms or a physical disorder (like Tiffany's TMD) that stem from a mental disorder? Or vice-versa: Have you experienced mental symptoms from a physical disease or disorder?

5: WHAT I LEARNED IN THERAPY

1. Have you tried any of the three relaxation techniques covered in this chapter? To what extent are they helpful for you?

Challenge: Try each of the techniques in this chapter!

2. What other helpful strategies or tips would you add to this chapter?

3. Do any of the four cognitive distortions highlighted in this chapter resonate with you? Which ones? Can you share any examples from your life?

Challenge: Do a little research to find a more comprehensive list of cognitive distortions and reflect on the questions above again.

4. How can identifying your own cognitive distortions benefit your mental health?

Challenge: Cognitive journaling is a helpful tool for overcoming cognitive distortions. Give it a try using the template and examples from the book and/or at **tiffanyciccone.com.**

5. Have you tried any kinds of counseling and/or therapy? If so, what kinds? How beneficial were they for you?

6. At this point in your life, do you think you might benefit from professional help of some sort? If so, what do you think your first steps would be? Would you like help or accountability?

6: VERSE

1. Do you currently journal or have you in the past? How often, and why?

2. Which of the three poems resonate most with you? (You can also fast-forward to page 178, where you can find a fourth one, "Jesus Was Lonely, Too.")

3. "Hyper and Restless and Lost" refers to a moment when simple words spoken from a stage sunk deeply into Tiffany's soul. Think of a time you experienced a moment of clarity or epiphany that brought you much-needed comfort or peace. It could have been sparked by the words of anyone, or simply by the Holy Spirit. Consider sharing your experience with the group.

4. Tiffany refers to lyrics in her poem that provide language for own experience. Do you have lyrics, quotes, or scripture that you cling to because they understand you?

Challenge: Try writing your own version of "Weak":

I used to think I _____.
Instead it turns out I'm _____.
But all the while I'm _____.
because God _____.

CHAPTER 7: MEDICATION

1. Has medication played a role in your mental health journey? How did/does it affect your spiritual life?

2. Whose medication journey do you relate to most: Julio's, April's, or Tiffany's? In what way(s)? Do you have any takeaways from their experiences?

3. Did this chapter change, challenge, or affirm your perspective on psychiatric medication?

4. If you take psychiatric medication, how open are you about it with other people, and why?

CHAPTER 8: VERSION 2.0

1. Have you ever experienced free-floating anxiety? If so, how do you cope with it?

2. The post by Scott Erickson gave Tiffany hope in the middle of her dry, fruitless season. What scriptures, quotes, or art do you cling to in difficult seasons?

Challenge: Print or handwrite some of your favorites onto paper (maybe even pretty paper!) and stick them where you will see them often. I've posted my faves next to my desk, above my dresser, and in my bathroom!

3. Have you ever asked someone to pray for your anxiety, depression, or other mental health struggle? If yes, how'd it go? If not, why not?

Challenge: The next time you're *going through it,* reach out to someone (or everyone) in your discussion group to ask for prayer and anything else that might help you.

4. What factors play into people's decisions to self-medicate? Do you struggle with self-medicating? Do you struggle with judging others for doing it?

5. If you've pursued professional care in the past, what obstacles or barriers did you encounter, if any? Did you end up getting the help you needed?

6. Have you wanted to pursue professional help before, but didn't? What prevented you from doing it?

CHAPTER 9: OVER OVERCOMING

1. Have you ever asked God "why"? Share about your experience.

2. Has the Prosperity Gospel affected your understanding of God and/or life (now or in the past)? How so?

3. Consider your prayer life in light of Jesus's prayer in Gethsemane:

    - Do you freely and fully express your pain (mental, emotional, physical) to God?
    - Do you tell Him what you long for?
    - Do you submit your will to His?

4. Tiffany mentioned that Jesus "not only changed eternity, but modeled how to suffer well." How well do you understand what it means that "Jesus changed eternity"? Explain in your own words, and discuss with others to come to an ever stronger understanding. She refers to the cross as God's way to "deal with humanity's problem of sin." What does this mean, and why is it relevant to our lives today?

CHAPTER 10: REDEMPTION: THE POWER OF WEAKNESS

1. After lamenting his thorn, Paul reflects on God's redemption of it. Have you gotten any glimpses of how God's redeeming your thorn for good? Share with the group.

2. As you look back on your life, can you see any possible benefits of God's answer of "no" to something you prayed for? What can you see in hindsight that you couldn't see at the time?

3. Recall the redemptive aspects of GAD that Tiffany discussed in this chapter. Have you experienced any similar benefits from struggles, weaknesses, or difficulties

you've been through?

4. In this chapter, Tiffany shares, "It's not about being strong; it's about being loved by the One who helps me in my weakness. It's about God's belief that I'm worth His time, worth 'riding through the skies and on the clouds' for." Do you believe this for yourself?

CHAPTER 11: SPEAKING OF STIGMA

1. Discuss one or more times you were on the giving or receiving end of stigma.

2. Who do you most want to understand your mental illness (or something else about you)? What is it that you wished they understood?

Challenge: Where words fail, prayer still works. When feeling misunderstood, pray that the Spirit reveals Truth in His timing, and then take refuge in God's perfect understanding of you.

3. How open are you about your thorn with others? Who do you talk to about it? Who is helpful, and who have you ruled out?

4. How can people best help you when you're feeling anxious (or depressed or...)?

5. Share about a time you had the opportunity to help someone with their anxiety. What did you do? Do you feel like you were able to be helpful? Is there anything you'd do differently in the future?

CHAPTER 12: SUNDAY MORNINGS

1. Have you ever belonged to a local church, either now or in the past? If you did in the past but not the present, why did you stop? Are you open or interested in getting to know a community of faith?

2. Has your anxiety ever been triggered during a religious gathering or event?

3. In what ways are church (or other social) gatherings or events challenging for you? What keeps you coming back despite the challenges?

4. Which Sunday morning challenges of Tiffany's resonate most with you?

CHAPTER 13: SERVING

1. Have you ever served or volunteered with a church or another organization? How important is that work to you and why?

2. Has your mental health ever prevented you from participating in something important to you? How do you cope with that?

3. What are ways you *can* participate in your local church during difficult seasons when you can't show up too much?

4. Have you noticed a time of day, week, month, or year that tends to be more difficult for you? If so, how do you brace yourself, adjust, and/or prepare for it?

5. To what extent does your self-worth depend on your usefulness? In other words, to what extent is your identity rooted in what you do as opposed to who you are? What is true of your identity in Christ?

CHAPTER 14: BELONGING AND THE BODY

1. Do you know of anyone who shares your faith and your diagnosis? It might be someone you follow on social media, a blogger, author, pastor, musician, etc.

2. Do you have a personal friendship with anyone who shares your faith and your diagnosis? What's that friendship like and how valuable is it to you?

Challenge: If you answered "no" to #1 and/or #2, visit **tiffanyciccone.com** for links to content by Christians who openly struggle with their mental health. You can also find links to organizations and supportive communities and resources at the intersection of faith and mental illness.

3. To what extent do you feel a sense of belonging in the Church?

4. What could other people do to help you feel like you belong?

5. How can you help others develop a sense of belonging or connection?

Cognitive Journal Template

COGNITIVE JOURNAL TEMPLATE

1 **Identify your feeling and rate its intensity from 1-100:**

2 **Identify the situation you were in when the feeling started:**

3 **Write out your automatic thoughts.** *Really call them out. Let them sound as extreme as they are.*

4 **Evidence that the automatic thought is true.** *Most garbage has a speck of truth in it. Find it by combing through what you wrote in step 3.*

5   **Evidence that the automatic thought is not 100% true.** *Comb through your automatic thoughts again. Then, write to challenge them, writing as much counter-evidence as you can.*

6   **More balanced thought** *Refer to the evidence it's true (step 4) and the evidence it's not 100% true (step 5) to write this part. It's also helpful to label any cognitive distortions.*

7   **Updated feeling with rating** *Don't expect a zero right away, because the physical manifestation of anxiety can take a while for the body to process.*

COGNITIVE JOURNAL EXAMPLE

1. **Identify your feeling and rate its intensity from 1-100.**

   Anxious: 70

2. **Identify the situation you were in when the feeling started.**

   Standing in the toothpaste aisle at Target, trying to decide which kind to buy.

3. **Write out your automatic thoughts.** *Really call them out. Let them sound as extreme as they are.*

   I'm going to disappoint God by choosing the wrong toothpaste. If I buy the pricey kind, then God will be upset with me because I'm not using the money to help His kids who don't have clean drinking water. But if I choose the cheap generic, then I'm failing to take care of the body God gave me. I'm going to do the wrong thing and ruin everything and disappoint the One I most want to please.

4. **Evidence that the automatic thought is true.** *Most garbage has a speck of truth in it. I find it by combing through what I wrote in "automatic thoughts."*

   Evidence it's true: Jesus does have a heart for the poor. He calls us to care for those who can't care for themselves. There are lots of people in the world who can't provide themselves with clean water, and I do have some money I can donate to help them. We are also called to take care of our bodies.

5. **Evidence that the automatic thought is not 100% true.** *To do this, I comb through my automatic thoughts again. Then, I write to challenge them, oftentimes piece by piece. Write as much counter-evidence as you need to. Sometimes it takes a while to get to the part that is really keeping me in the whirlpool.*

   Evidence it's NOT 100% true: God can make water come from rocks, like in Old Testament times. He does not need to depend or rely on me to make it happen. He knows I can't save the world. I can't even save myself. He saves me, and then He lovingly invites me to participate in His work, like a parent who invites their three year old to stir the batter. He doesn't give me the butcher knife—more responsibility than I'm ready for.

And the toothpaste I buy doesn't have to determine whether or not I donate to an organization that gives kids clean water. I can do both.

6. **More balanced thought.** *I refer to the evidence it's true (step 4) and the evidence it's not 100% true (step 5) to write this part. It's also helpful to label any cognitive distortions.*

God is looking down on me in compassion right now, not in hot disappointment. My choice won't surprise Him. The way I'm struggling doesn't either.

This is a cognitive distortion: a blend of all-or-nothing thinking and catastrophic thinking. Catastrophe will not unfold because of this tiny act of mine. I am not that powerful. God doesn't give His kids more responsibility than they're ready for. He won't enable me to foil His plans. He is a Good Father, and He protects me from myself.

7. **Updated feeling with rating** *Don't expect a zero right away, because the physical manifestation of anxiety can take a while for the body to process. I started at 70, so 30's not bad at all!*

Anxious: 30.

COGNITIVE JOURNAL EXAMPLE

1 **Identify your feeling and rate its intensity from 1-100.**

Anxious: 30

2 **Identify the situation you were in when the feeling started.**

At Restored early. I didn't excitedly greet Pastor Danny or my friend Brandon.

3 **Write out your automatic thoughts.** *Really call them out. Let them sound as extreme as they are.*

I'm terrible. I can't even show love or encouragement to my pastor or my friend. I'm ruining their mornings. They care for me so well and now they think I don't care at all. Now they're discouraged and I suck.

4 **Evidence that the automatic thought is true.** *Most garbage has a speck of truth in it. I find it by combing through what I wrote in "automatic thoughts."*

When I first saw them I didn't excitedly hug them in "OMG" fashion. They do care about me.

5 **Evidence that the automatic thought is not 100% true.** *To do this, I comb through my automatic thoughts again. Then, I write to challenge them, oftentimes piece by piece. Write as much counter-evidence as you need to. Sometimes it takes a while to get to the part that is really keeping me in the whirlpool.*

Their worlds don't rely on me. I am not the center of their hearts. God is. Their state of being depends on Jesus, it is never ultimately on me. What I do or say doesn't ruin them. God is their center. I am not that powerful.

6 More balanced thought. *I refer to the evidence it's true (step 4) and the evidence it's not 100% true (step 5) to write this part. It's also helpful to label any cognitive distortions.*

My natural disposition isn't to jump up and down when I greet people. And I'm not one of those super confidant people who assumes others want attention from. That's something Jesus may want to work on me regarding. But peoples well being is not on me. They don't revolve around my action or inaction. Everything is okay. Everything is fine. Danny and Brandon know me and don't expect me to greet them with a ton of gusto. They know I have other ways of caring, and besides, I'm not in control of their inner world.

Cognitive distortions: mind reading, emotional reasoning. Catastrophizing.

7 Updated feeling with rating. *Don't expect a zero right away, because the physical manifestation of anxiety can take a while for the body to process. I started at 30, so 10's not bad at all!*

Anxious: 10.

END NOTES

INTRO

1 Matthew 6:26

2 Philippians 4:7 ESV

3 James 1:19 CSB

CHAPTER 1

1 M. Bekkhus Et al., "Developmental changes in the structure of shyness and internalizing symptoms from early to middle childhood: A network analysis." *Society for Research in Child Development*, (2023), 94(4), 1078-1086. https://doi.org/10.1111/cdev.13906.

2 "Generalized Anxiety Disorder," Perelman School of Medicine at the University of Pennsylvania, https://www.med.upenn.edu/ctsa/general_anxiety_symptoms.html.

3 Elizabeth A. Hoge, Julia E. Oppenheimer, and Naomi M. Simon, "Generalized Anxiety Disorder," *FOCUS: the Journal of Lifelong Learning in Psychiatry* 2, no. 3 (July 1, 2004): 346–59, https://doi.org/10.1176/foc.2.3.346.

4 Lori Gallimore, Kathryn Conrad, and University of Tennessee, *Understanding Disabilities: Anxiety in Children and Youth*, https://utia.tennessee.edu/publications/wp-content/uploads/sites/269/2023/10/W947-G.pdf.

5 Thomas S. Monson

6 "America Has Reached Peak Therapy: Why Is Our Mental Health Getting Worse?" *Time Magazine*, Aug. 28, 2023.

7 Vivek H. Murthy and U.S. Surgeon General, *Protecting Youth Mental Health: The U.S. Surgeon General's Advisory*, 2021, https://www.hhs.gov/sites/default/files/surgeon-general-youth-mental-health-advisory.pdf.

8 "Generalized Anxiety Disorder," American Academy of Family Physicians, Dec. 6, 2022, https://familydoctor.org/condition/generalized-anxiety-disorder/.

CHAPTER 2

1 Matthew 6:34

2 Philippians 4:6-7

3 Hebrews 12:2

4 Philippians 4:4

5 The origin of this piano is a hallmark of our childhood. We were visiting my great-grandmother when she told my brother, sister, and I that we could have anything we wanted. I, at age seven, asked for a painting easel. My sister, at five, wanted a grand piano. Our brother, who was three, asked for a coloring book. We each got what we wanted. We still laugh about it. Except for my brother.

6 Five Iron Frenzy, "Four-Fifty-One." *All the Hype That Money Can Buy*. 5 Minute Walk, 2000.

7 Mark 16:15

8 Philippians 4:4

9 Matthew 6:19

10 Ephesians 2:8-9

CHAPTER 3

1 Matthew 23:24

2 Justin later coached me through writing this book! He also led worship in Mexico on my 9th grade mission trip to Mexico with Harvest.

3 Re-reading this convinced me to write some for this book, too.

4 1 Corinthians 9:22

5 Acts 17:26

6 John 17:14-15

7 Ezekiel 36:26-27

CHAPTER 4

1 "Generalized Anxiety Disorder (Symptoms)," Perelman School of Medicine at the University of Pennsylvania, https://www.med.upenn.edu/ctsa/general_anxiety_symptoms.html.

2 "Generalized Anxiety Disorder - Symptoms and Causes," Mayo Clinic, Oct. 13, 2017, https://www.mayoclinic.org/diseases-conditions/generalized-anxiety-disorder/symptoms-causes/syc-20360803.

3 "Diagnosis and Management of Generalized Anxiety Disorder and Panic Disorder in Adults," PubMed, May 1, 2015, https://pubmed.ncbi.nlm.nih.gov/25955736/.

4 "Anxiety Disorders - Symptoms and Causes," Mayo Clinic, May 4, 2018, https://www.mayoclinic.org/diseases-conditions/anxiety/symptoms-causes/syc-20350961.

5 "Chronic Pain," Anxiety & Depression Association of America, Aug. 10, 2023, https://adaa.org/understanding-anxiety/related-illnesses/other-related-conditions/

chronic-pain.

6 Jacob Louis, Et al. "Association between carpal tunnel syndrome and the five-year incidence of anxiety disorder and depression in adults followed in general practices in Germany," *Journal of Psychosomatic Research* 173 (October 2023), https://www.sciencedirect.com/science/article/abs/pii/S0022399923003264.

7 Proverbs 16:9

8 Matthew 16:24

9 Philippians 4:7

10 James 1:27

CHAPTER 5

1 John 9:6-7

2 Mark 8:22-26

3 "Learning Diaphragmatic Breathing," Harvard Health, March 10, 2016, https://www.health.harvard.edu/healthbeat/learning-diaphragmatic-breathing.

4 Elizabeth Hartney BSc, MSc, MA, PhD, "10 Cognitive Distortions That Can Cause Negative Thinking," *Verywell Mind*, November 8, 2023, https://www.verywellmind.com/ten-cognitive-distortions-identified-in-cbt-22412.

5 "What Is OCD & Scrupulosity?" International OCD Foundation, December 15, 2022, https://iocdf.org/faith-ocd/what-is-ocd-scrupulosity/.

6 The explanation of each cognitive distortion is adapted from *The Feeling Good Handbook* by David D. Burns, MD.

7 Proverbs 27:17

CHAPTER 6

1 Five Iron Frenzy, "See the Flames Begin to Crawl" on *The End Is Near*

2 Brave Saint Saturn, "Invictus." *Anti-Meridian.* Department of Biophysics, 2008. https://youtu.be/t5eeQafidEQ?si=EP5mjZqfCp8oe_4X.

3 Psalm 78:39

CHAPTER 7

1 Matthew 16:25

2 Luke 22:42

3 Psalm 139:2

4 Hebrews 13:5

5 Luke 10:27

CHAPTER 8

1 Kendra Cherry MSEd, "What Is Free-Floating Anxiety?" *Verywell Mind*, July 25, 2022, https://www.verywellmind.com/free-floating-anxiety-definition-symptoms-traits-causes-treatment-511662

2 C.S. Lewis, "Learning in War-Time." *The Weight of Glory* (New York, NY: Harper Collins, 1949), 61.

3 Scott Erickson (@scottthepainter), Our great mistake is to use language to describe our lives as binary, Feb. 9, 2020, https://www.instagram.com/p/B8WfiZwp5v4/?utm_source=ig_web_copy_link&igsh=MTI2bDBiYWszdDM4bA==.

4 Galatians 6:2

5 Five Iron Frenzy. "So Far." *Engine of a Million Plots.* Department of Biophysics, 2013, https://youtu.be/2qEB4tspw1g?si=AEeXZSXw54tRkAvb.

6 Horatio Spafford, "It Is Well with My Soul," 1873.

The history of the song is compelling: Learn about it here:

https://seelemag.com/home/story-behind-it-is-well-with-my-soul-cportee#google_vignette=.

7 Mark 11:15-18

8 Origin unknown. Some sources indicate John Bradford.

9 Beth Salcedo, MD. "The Comorbidity of Anxiety and Depression, "National Alliance on Mental Illness, Jan. 19, 2018, https://www.nami.org/education/the-comorbidity-of-anxiety-and-depression/.

CHAPTER 9

1 2 Corinthians 12:8

2 Psalms 34:18

3 Hebrews 13:5-6, Deuteronomy 31:6

4 Romans 8:26-27

5 Romans 8:35-39

6 Luke 1:38

7 2 Corinthians 12:7

8 Check out my friend Adrian's brand at weallugly.com!

9 Acts 9

10 2 Corinthians 11: 23-29

11 James 1:2

12 Thomas Turner, "Stop Taking Jeremiah 29:11 Out of Context," *Relevant Magazine,* Nov. 13, 2024, https://relevantmagazine.com/faith/stop-taking-jeremiah-2911-out-context/.

13 John 15:20, John 16:33, Matthew 16:24 respectively

14 Isaiah 53

15 Inspired by this song: Justin McRoberts, "But You Called

Me," *Curse of the Faithful* EP, May 5, 2020, https://youtu.be/6UT8-tjvQyU?si=sC9ddeHyOvmx9osk.

16 James 4:14, Psalm 144:4, Job 14:2

17 Romans 5:3-5

18 Mark 14:32-26

19 Luke 22:43-44

20 Matthew 27:46

21 Hebrews 12:2

CHAPTER 10

1 C.S. Lewis, *Present Concerns: Journalistic Essays,* "On Living in an Atomic Age," (C.S. Lewis Ptd. Ltd., 1986).

2 Matthew 7:26

3 Proverbs 18:24, John 15:15

4 Isaiah 53:3

5 Hebrews 4:15

6 Proverbs 16:18

7 Romans 3:23

8 Deuteronomy 33:26-27a

9 See Psalm 51, 69, 77, 86 and 142 for some of David's cries to God. For Elijah, see I Kings 19:3-9. For Hagar, see Gen. 21:14-20. For Moses, see Exodus.

CHAPTER 11

1 Acts 20:28-29

2 John 9:1-3

3 Philippians 4:6

4 This sentence is inspired by something written by one of my brilliant college besties, Evil Smell, LMFT.

CHAPTER 12

1 Hebrews 10:25

2 John 17:21-23a

3 1 John 3:16

4 Ephesians 5:21

5 1 Thessalonians 5:14

6 Galatians 6:2

7 Ephesians 5:19

8 From the Meyers-Briggs Personality test. You can take a free test at 16personalities.com.

CHAPTER 13

1 Matthew 6:1

2 Mark 12: 41-44

3 Ecclesiastes 3:1-8

4 Ephesians 2:10

5 Aaron Earls, "Pastors Have Congregational and, for Some, Personal Experience With Mental Illness." *Lifeway Research*, Aug. 2, 2022, https://research.lifeway.com/2022/08/02/pastors-have-congregational-and-for-some-personal-experience-with-mental-illness/.

6 Mark 6:7

7 Philippians 4:11-13

CHAPTER 14

1 Romans 7:20

2 John 16:13

3 2 Corinthians 12:9-10

4 1 Corinthians 12:21-26

5 Luke 8:22-25; Matthew 8:23-27; Mark 4:35-41

About the Author

Tiffany Ciccone isn't sure what to write here. In the past, she'd say she's an English Teacher, and in the future, she'll say she's a therapist. Right now, she's a child of God (like you) who's publishing her first book, waiting for grad school to start, and volunteering with Young Life. She loves playing in her garden, listening to bad music, and exploring San Diego where she lives with her husband, Patrick; pup, Madison; and their friend, Brenda.

VISIT TIFFANY AT:

- tiffanyciccone.com.
- instagram.com/tiffany.ciccone
- substack.com/@tiffanyciccone

www.ingramcontent.com/pod-product-compliance
Lightning Source LLC
Chambersburg PA
CBHW070619030426
42337CB00020B/3853